Unveilin
Feast of Wee.

MW01242002

By Ron C. Harmon

Tomorrow's Church of God
Temple Texas

Contact us
www.thetcog.com

tomorrowtcog@gmail.com

Chapters for quick reference

Unveiling the Omer
Feast of Weeks or Pentecost

What's Truth Worth?

Luke 8:17, *For nothing is hidden that will not become evident, nor anything secret that will not be known and come to light.*

Any book worth its weight in salt always starts with a good subject or premise artfully guiding the narrative throughout the entire conversation. The premise of this book is based upon one question aimed at all claiming to know God and His will. A question that followers of the true Messiah must also come to terms with at some time during their lifelong spiritual journey is, "Are we willing to take any step necessary to separate ourselves completely from the world?"

A simple question based upon a passage found in the revelations of John, *I heard another voice from heaven, saying, "Come out of her, my people, so that you will not participate in her sins and receive any of her plagues (**Revelation 18:4**).*

The knee-jerk response would be a resounding "yes" from most believers, especially if one thinks of himself or herself as a disciple of the truth. But one should be asking themselves, "is that simply my religious auto-response kicking in as a Christian?" Almost weekly or even daily, those who believe they're chosen by God are told they have successfully come out of the world. But it's funny how actions and beliefs dictate something entirely different about so-called believers in the secular world.

It also seemed obvious to the writer of **Proverbs 14:12**, where he made the observation, *12 There is a way that seems right to a man, But its end is the way of death. NKJV*

This same sentiment is repeated in **Proverbs 16:25**, NKJV, *There is a way that seems right to a man, But its end is the way of death.*

Feeling safe and secure in one's beliefs is the essence of a warm fuzzy gift from Satan. What do I mean by that? Man tends to remain in Satan's clutches while entertaining the idea they're basking in God's light of truth. This is designed by Satan, entrapping the believer's mind into thinking they have one foot in the door of God's kingdom while he is clutching their coat tails.

Despite the nearly impossible task of extricating oneself from Satan's grasp, it's still one's duty to the Eternal to continuously try despite the enormous barriers. It's a Godly task dedicating one's self to the Eternal, even though old and newly formed traditions present insurmountable obstacles.

There are times in a believer's life where slivers of truth filter down through the cracks of our traditions bringing new never seen before light. This may have happened to some in the beginning of understanding God's ways. Rays of truth may once have led some to give up old traditions like Christmas, Easter, and other secular traditions. Giving up these may seem like child's play compared to some long-standing hidden biblical traditions a believer must also overcome. Believers may be completely unaware of these hidden biblical traditions even though they've been a member of one of God's churches for decades.

Becoming Biblically oriented, initiates a beginning of subtle transformation inside a believer's mind, causing an unfathomable desire to know truth. Suddenly, all the misinformation previously taught seems glaringly apparent, causing anger, and challenging a believer to seek clarification and change if necessary. God's truths once cloaked in deception by Satan become exposed to light from the Bible, change is inevitable…. willingly or not.

An inquisitive mind holds the key to opening the door to wondrous teachings. Sadly, we don't see everything in the beginning; it takes years to make sense of all God's glorious truths. Even though God's truths lay exposed on the surface of the pages of the Bible, most believers can't resist substituting traditions in place of truth. It's what we do as humans; we are naturally programmed to love and honor our traditions above all else. Traditions are man's mistress taking our attention away from the one we should be devoted to, God. Traditions whisper in the believer's ear not to worry whether you're doing the right things….she (traditions) is always there to comfort the believer.

The comfortability factor is the second reason folks don't fully come to terms with keeping one foot in the world. Believers are programmed not to rock the boat; it tends to upset the equilibrium of their religious convictions. Leaving family and friends behind for a new doctrine is often too much for the human psychic. Risking all for an intangible God isn't worth it for many; better to suffer a perceived wrath than lose one's standing in the world.

Combining old traditions with comfortability gives Satan a powerful psychological tool he uses to hide and work against believers. The same reason Satan feels comfortable in the shadows is the same reason that causes God's people to feel safe and comfortable within their beliefs. It's a circle of death trapping the minds by the billions and keeping them from seeing even a little truth.

Even though a few successfully manage to leave the majority of the world behind, many are still influenced daily by old ways. Ways in the form of traditions unknowingly brought on the journey with them. Old ideas and traditions are the very reason for this book, so we, believers, can stand together and help each other recognize this unwanted and sometimes hidden baggage.

This is an effort to disregard old influences and give over to the new creature God creates within the man or woman. Dark and light cannot mix, the same as evil and good cannot mix, so the new creature can't grow feeding on old ways.

Our habit of holding onto the old self appears at times as a passive form of insanity and is indefensible for a believer. It's this insanity causing good folks to succumb to instances of ungodly anger at the very mention they may be wrong. This happens when they come face to face with those they disagree with concerning doctrine. It's an inexplicable reaction to a new or different understanding of the scriptures. Our protective nature wants to lash out at the invading issues attempting to drive the comfortable from our lives.

It's as if the mind is rejecting the words while clinging onto the last vestiges of their once-certain lives. Even if one has fought spiritual battles in the past over different doctrines that separate them from other churches, they still have this reaction when taking the next step in that journey.

It's a believer's constant battle to get both feet into God's kingdom while leaving this world in the rearview mirror. Although we are to work out our salvation, seeking help doesn't hurt when clarification is needed.

That leads me back to the beginning and the next step.

The Next Step

1 John 4:1, *Beloved, do not believe every spirit, but test the spirits to see whether they are from God. For many false prophets have gone out into the world.*

I harken back to the Saturday mornings of my childhood; we would gather around the television to watch Bugs Bunny, Daffy Duck, Foghorn Leghorn, and all the other cartoon characters. I, my brothers and sisters, spent two or three hours watching and enjoying the antics played out in front of our eyes. One of my favorites was the roadrunner and coyote, and it never failed to entertain me how the roadrunner always got the best of the persistent coyote.

Many of these cartoon scenarios included a character going over a ledge and hanging helplessly under incredible conditions which normal humans couldn't sustain. The effort not to let go seemed effortless, but we all knew that even if the character fell, he would never be seriously hurt. Often, a twig or one finger kept the character from falling what seemed like miles to the canyon floor below and landing in a cloud of smoke or dust.

The same scenario seems to be playing out concerning scripture and the hidden truths of God's word. People love their traditions so much they hang on tooth and nail, sometimes by a twig, not giving in to apparent truth.

This same persistence is more than evident with doctrines of the Feast of Weeks (Shavuot) versus Pentecost. In this instance, the cartoon character's twig of safety is the word "Sabbath" in Leviticus 23:11 & 15.

For those comfortable with the Christian Pentecost traditions, **Leviticus 23:11** is the weekly "Sabbath," and that's

where to begin counting; let's read the NASB version of the passage in question for the purpose of clarification. We'll start in verse 9. *Then the Eternal spoke to Moses, saying, 10. "Speak to the sons of Israel and say to them, 'When you enter the land which I am going to give to you and you gather its harvest, then you shall bring in the sheaf of the first fruits of your harvest to the Priest. 11. He shall wave the sheaf before the Eternal for you to be accepted; on the day after the **Sabbath** the Priest shall wave it. 12. Now on the Day when you wave the sheaf, you shall offer a male lamb one year old without defect as a burnt offering to the Eternal. 13. Its grain offering shall then be two-tenths of an ephah of fine flour mixed with oil, an offering by fire to the Eternal for a soothing aroma, with its drink offering, a fourth of a hin of wine. 14. Until this very day, until you have brought in the offering of your God, you shall eat neither bread nor roasted grain nor new produce. It is to be a permanent statute throughout your generations in all your dwelling places. 15. You shall also count for yourselves from the day after the **Sabbath**, from the day when you brought in the sheaf of the wave offering; there shall be seven complete **Sabbaths**. 16. You shall count fifty days to the day after the seventh Sabbath; then you shall present a new grain offering to the Eternal.*
(Leviticus 23:9-16)

As I previously stated, the word sabbath used in this passage has been a linchpin within the church for eons and isn't going to fade away any time soon despite the best efforts of some.

"What difference does this definition make?" You might be thinking.

The difference is whether we are keeping one foot in the world or trying to get both in the kingdom of God. So, realizing there may be some folks unaware there is a difference between

Feast of Weeks and Pentecost, I'll lay out the arguments on both sides to answer that question for everyone's benefit. This isn't about what I sincerely believe in my heart but digging into the roots of a subject for proper discernment.

Viewing the word Sabbath in Lev. 23:11 & 15 as the 7th day of observance is the traditional guidepost for modern churches claiming you begin counting 50 days after the weekly Sabbath, which occurs within the days of Unleavened Bread. Doing this will put you on a Sunday observance of one of God's holy days every year without exception.

The opposite interpretation says the word Sabbath means more than just the 7th day; it also means an annual holy day, specifically the 1st day of Unleavened Bread. So, taking that into account, one would begin counting fifty days from the day AFTER celebrating the 1st Day of Unleavened Bread, often referred to as the 2nd day of Passover. By counting from this day, it places the Feast of Weeks or Pentecost 50 days later and falls on any day of the week, and not just on a Sunday.

You see, it's just that one word, and you might think it would be easy to overcome…. but not so fast with that assumption. Believers, saying it's the 7th day Sabbath, seem to be persistent in killing the idea that Sabbath can mean an annual high day the same as the coyote is at catching the roadrunner. Surely, there is proof somewhere out there that will put this disagreement to bed once and for all. You would be mistaken, not because there isn't any proof of the meaning of the word used in Lev. 23:11, but because of the cliffhanger effect.

I'll be upfront here and admit I fall on the side of the word Sabbath being the 1st Day of Unleavened Bread, and this book has a lot to do with why I believe what I believe. I said there was proof, and I'll be happy to back up what I say, so please follow along.

To begin with, the word Sabbath in Lev. 23:11 isn't a bad word…I won't even say it's an incorrect word. But to understand the context, we must first thoroughly understand the definition of the word "Sabbath." After all, this is the twig our friends on the other side of the issue are clinging onto…. Seemingly, for life's sake.

Let's begin by checking Strong's Hebrew definition for every instance the word Sabbath is used in the Torah. I'll confine the parameters of my search to just the Torah for now, which should give us what we need. We can expand outward as needed, but the Torah (first five books) should be enough…for now.

When the word Sabbath is used, our minds naturally default to the 7th day observance, that's normal with any member of the churches of God. God's people understand God rested on the 7th day and sanctified it as a day of rest for man to observe as holy or "set apart."

By the seventh day God completed His work which He had done, and He rested on the seventh day from all His work which He had done. 3 Then God blessed the seventh day and sanctified it, because on it He rested from all His work which God had created and made. **(Genesis 2:2-3)**

The Eternal God made it an ordinance once He brought the children of Israel out of Egypt and to the promised land.

8 "Remember the Sabbath day, to keep it holy. 9 For six days you shall labor and do all your work, 10 but the seventh day is a Sabbath of the Eternal your God; on it you shall not do any work, you, or your son, or your daughter, your male slave or your female slave, or your cattle, or your resident who stays with you. 11 For in six days the Eternal made the heavens and the earth, the sea and everything that is in them, and He rested on the seventh day; for that reason the Eternal blessed the Sabbath day and made it holy. **(Exodus 20:8-11)**

At first glance, it would appear to bear witness to this being the weekly Sabbath in Lev. 23:11 & 15, or is there more to the word we've yet to explore?

I don't mean to sound arrogant or hateful, but believers often tell me they are better educated than I am and spend a lot of time researching extensively in prestigious libraries for correct meanings of words. As a result, they adamantly know this is the 7th day and can't possibly be an annual high day. As limited as my studies are, they say something much different, which I'm about to share. And, by limiting the scope of the word, we may be guilty of hindering the Eternal's will in these matters, something we must consider.

For instance, **Smith's Bible dictionary** defines the word (shabbath), *"a day of rest," from shabath "to cease to do to," "to rest"*).

Webster's 1828 Dictionary SABBATH noun *The Day which God appointed to be observed by the Jews as a day **of rest** from all secular labor or employments, and to be kept holy and consecrated to his service and worship.*

Unger's Bible Dictionary, SABBATH *(Heb. shabbāt, "repose," i.e., **"cessation" from exertion**; Gk. sabbaton). The name Sabbath is applied to various great festivals but principally and usually to the seventh day of the week, the strict observance of which is enforced not merely in the general Mosaic code but also in the Ten Commandments.*

Volumes of Biblical dictionaries or commentaries agree with the definition of the word "Sabbath" (from the Hebrew verb Shabbat, meaning **"to rest from labor"**.

It is a time when God ceased all work and rested and also a time when God told His people to cease work and rest.

If God says to rest on a day, it's a Sabbath, and it does not need to be exclusively on the 7th day. God's people don't have a problem calling any other Holy Days, High days, or Sabbaths, only when it comes to defining **Leviticus 23: 11 & 15**.

We can see this by going back to Leviticus 23 and reading the instructions surrounding the other holy days, including the weekly Sabbath.

Leviticus 23:1-3, *The Eternal spoke again to Moses, saying, 2. "Speak to the sons of Israel and say to them, 'The Eternal's appointed times which you shall proclaim as holy convocations—My appointed times are these:*
Weekly Sabbath *3. 'For six days work may be done, but on the seventh day there is a Sabbath of complete rest**, a holy convocation. You shall not do any work**; it is a Sabbath to the Eternal in all your dwellings.*

Yearly Festivals

Leviticus 23:4-8. *'These are the appointed times of the Eternal, holy convocations which you shall proclaim at the times appointed for them. 5. In the first month, on the fourteenth day of the month at twilight is the Eternal's Passover. 6. Then on the fifteenth day of the same month there is the Feast of Unleavened Bread to the Eternal; for seven days you shall eat unleavened bread. 7. **On the first day you shall have a holy convocation; you shall not do any laborious work**. 8. But for seven days you shall present an offering by fire to the Eternal. On the seventh day is a holy convocation; **you shall not do any laborious work.**'"*

We just read the first eight verses of Leviticus 23 and God's instructions to Moses was for Israel to cease from their work two additional times other than the weekly Sabbath. These are very specific instructions on observing the 1st and last Day of Unleavened Bread. Look at the instructions I have highlighted. They say to cease your labor, rest, and celebrate God with a holy convocation.

You say God is commanding a day of celebration by using the word convocation, but the same wording is also used for the weekly Sabbath…look at verse 3 of Leviticus 23, afterward, look at the rest of Leviticus 23….

Leviticus 23:9-22, *Then the Eternal spoke to Moses, saying, 10. "Speak to the sons of Israel and say to them, 'When you enter the land which I am going to give to you and you gather its harvest, then you shall bring in the sheaf of the first fruits of your harvest to the Priest. 11. He shall wave the sheaf before the Eternal for you to be accepted; on the day after the Sabbath the Priest shall wave it. 12. Now on the Day when you wave the sheaf, you shall offer a male lamb one year old without defect as a burnt offering to the Eternal. 13. Its grain offering shall then be two-tenths of an ephah of fine flour mixed with oil, an offering by fire to the Eternal for a soothing aroma, with its drink offering, a fourth of a hin of wine. 14 Until this very day, until you have brought in the offering of your God, you shall eat neither bread nor roasted grain nor new produce. It is to be a permanent statute throughout your generations in all your dwelling places.*
15 'You shall also count for yourselves from the day after the Sabbath, from the day when you brought in the sheaf of the wave offering; there shall be seven complete Sabbaths. 16 You shall count fifty days to the day after the seventh Sabbath; then you shall present a new grain offering to the Eternal. 17 You shall bring in from your dwelling places two loaves of bread as a wave offering, made of two-tenths of an ephah; they shall be

*of a fine flour, baked with leaven as first fruits to the Eternal.
18 Along with the bread you shall present seven one-year-old
male lambs without defect, and a bull of the herd and two rams;
they are to be a burnt offering to the Eternal, with their grain
offering and their drink offerings, an offering by fire of a
soothing aroma to the Eternal. 19. You shall also offer one
male goat as a sin offering, and two male lambs one year old as
a sacrifice of peace offerings. 20. The Priest shall then wave
them with the bread of the first fruits as a wave offering with
two lambs before the Eternal; they are to be holy to the Eternal
for the Priest. 21. On this very day you shall make a
proclamation as well; you are to have a holy convocation.* **You
shall do no laborious work.** *It is to be a permanent statute in
all your dwelling places throughout your generations.
22. 'When you reap the harvest of your land, moreover, you
shall not reap to the very edges of your field nor gather the
gleaning of your harvest; you are to leave them for the needy
and the stranger. I am the Eternal your God.'"*

Feast of Trumpets

Leviticus 23:23-35, *Again the Eternal spoke to Moses, saying,
24 "Speak to the sons of Israel, saying, 'In the seventh month
on the first of the month you shall have a rest, a reminder by
blowing of trumpets,* **a holy convocation. 25. You shall not do
any laborious work**, *but you shall present an offering by fire to
the Eternal.'"*

The Day of Atonement

Leviticus 23:26-32, *Then the Eternal spoke to Moses, saying,
27. "On exactly the tenth day of this seventh month is the Day*

*of Atonement; it shall be a holy convocation for you, and you shall humble yourselves and present an offering by fire to the Eternal. 28. You shall not do any work on this very day, for it is a Day of Atonement, to make atonement on your behalf before the Eternal your God. 29. If there is any person who does not humble himself on this very day, he shall be cut off from his people. 30. As for any person who does any work on this very day, that person I will eliminate from among his people. 31. You shall not do any work. It is to be a permanent statute throughout your generations in all your dwelling places. 32. It is to be a **Sabbath of complete rest for you**, and you shall humble yourselves; on the ninth of the month at evening, from evening until evening, **you shall keep your Sabbath.***"

The word Sabbath is used here as a definition of the day. I've been told the meaning of the word Sabbath in this instance is not the same word as the word in Lev. 23:11, but looking both up in Strong's, the Hebrew definition for both instances says they are the same word and mean the same thing.

Using **Strong's Hebrew**, both are defined as the number *7676 having the base root in 7673, which says. 7673 shabath shaw-bath' a primitive root; to repose, i.e. desist from exertion; used in many implied relations (causative, figurative or specific):--(**cause to, let, make to) cease**, celebrate, cause (make) to fail, keep (Sabbath), suffer to be lacking, leave, put away (down), (**make to) rest**, rid, still, take away.*

For context, here is the Strong's Hebrew definition of the number **7676**, shabbath shab-bawth' intensive from **7673**; intermission, i.e (specifically) the Sabbath: --(+ every) sabbath.

To be even more precise, I searched diligently for a different definition of the word Sabbath being used anywhere else in the Torah or Old Testament in its entirety, and all have the same definition, (*a day of rest or cessation of work*).

There is one exception having more to do with the length of time of the Sabbath period. That has to do with the Sabbatical year mentioned in **Exodus 23:10-11**, *"Now you shall sow your land for six years and gather in its yield, 11. but in the seventh year* **you shall let it rest and lie uncultivated**, *so that the needy of your people may eat; and whatever they leave the animal of the field may eat. You are to do the same with your vineyard and your olive grove.*

As we see, the definition didn't change, it was still a time set aside for rest, only the length of time referenced in the parameters by God.

Let's continue through the 23rd chapter of Leviticus and the rest of God's annual holy days.

Feast of Tabernacles

Leviticus 23:33-36, *Again the Eternal spoke to Moses, saying, 34. "Speak to the sons of Israel, saying, 'On the fifteenth of this seventh month is the Feast of Booths for seven days to the Eternal. 35. On* **the first day is a holy convocation; you shall not do any laborious work**. *36. For seven days you shall present an offering by fire to the Eternal. On the eighth day you shall have a* **holy convocation** *and present an offering by fire to the Eternal; it is an assembly.* **You shall not do any laborious work.**

The following are two verses we need to take particular interest in because they point out something which has been glossed over for years.

Leviticus 23:37-38, *'These are the appointed times of the Eternal which you shall proclaim* **as holy convocations**, *to present offerings by fire to the Eternal—burnt offerings and grain offerings, sacrifices and drink offerings, each day's* *matter on its own day— 38. **besides those of the Sabbaths of the Eternal**, and besides your gifts and besides all your vowed and voluntary offerings, which you give to the Eternal.*

To be more easily understood, let's read these two verses in another translation. This is the **living translation,** *37. "(These, then, are the regular annual festivals—**sacred convocations of all people**—when offerings to the Eternal are to be made by fire. 38. These **annual festivals** are in addition to your regular **Sabbaths**—the weekly days of holy rest. The sacrifices made during the festivals are to be in addition to your regular giving and normal fulfillment of your vows.)*

One more for verification as to what I'm about to point out…this is the **New Century Version (NCV) version** *37.* *("These are the Eternal's special feasts, when there will be holy meetings and when you bring offerings made by fire to the Eternal. You will bring whole burnt offerings, grain offerings, sacrifices, and drink offerings—each at the right time. 38. These offerings are in addition to those for the Eternal's Sabbath days, in addition to offerings you give as payment for special promises, and in addition to special offerings you want to give to the Eternal.)*

The writer (Moses) points out that the annual holy days and sacrifices are in addition to the weekly Sabbath.

Would those additions also include the definition of the word Sabbath? Because, as we have seen in the instructions for all the days mentioned are a cessation of work, a holy convocation is also to be included.

Reading the rest of Leviticus 23, the following is simply a reiteration of what we already have covered, other than to say they are statutes for all eternity.

So you shall celebrate it as a feast to the Eternal for seven days in the year. It shall be a permanent statute throughout your generations; you shall celebrate it in the seventh month. 42. You shall live in booths for seven days; all the native-born in Israel shall live in booths, 43 so that your generations may know that I had the sons of Israel live in booths when I brought them out from the land of Egypt. I am the Eternal your God.'" **44 So Moses declared to the sons of Israel the appointed times of the Eternal. (Leviticus 23:41-44)**

Are you beginning to feel an uncomfortable tug on the old brain? We aren't programmed to view the Sabbath beyond the boundaries set by CHRISTIAN churches. Our western thinking brains are in full TILT, considering Sabbath may have a definition outside of just one day of the week, that day being the 7th day of the week.

Let me ask those familiar with God's word and using the word Sabbath as a sign between Him and his people in **Exodus 31:12-17** and also in **Ezekiel 20:12**, where it says, *I also gave them my Sabbaths to be a sign between us so they would know that I am the Eternal who made them holy.*

After going through Leviticus 23 and seeing the same instructions associated with annual holy days, along with the weekly Sabbath, all are to be treated as holy convocations. My question is this, "does this mean the annual holy days are included in the sign God places upon His people?" Or instead, is only the 7th day God's sign of His people, excluding the annual holy days?

I do find it interesting the word Sabbaths is used in **Ezekiel 20:12**, meaning more than one. Does that mean all 52 weekly Sabbaths, including the annual holy days?

I hear you shouting, "What difference does it make?"

Here is the reason I point this out. If you say Sabbath means only the weekly 7th day Sabbath in **Leviticus 23:11**, denying it could also mean the annual 1st Day of Unleavened Bread, then you are also saying only the weekly 7thday Sabbath is a sign between God and His people.

    Meaning the annual holy days of God can't define God's people or be seen as separating them from the world. That's the most ridiculous reasoning, you might be thinking to yourself. We all know words mean things, and believers can't have it both ways. Either the weekly 7th day and the 7 annual holy days are a sign between God and His people, or the 7 annual holy days aren't a part of God's sign. As I have already pointed out Sabbath means the same in every instance, whether weekly or annual holy day. It's a day of rest, a day of ceasing from work to hold a holy convocation.

Sabbath in the New Testament

Mark 2:27, *"The sabbath was made for man, and not man for the sabbath"*

Does Sabbath in the New Testament mean the same as Sabbath in the Old Testament? I ask because I've been told the language is different, and therefore the meaning of the word is different.

As Sherlock Holmes would say, "Watson, let's investigate and get to the bottom of this conundrum."

Let's begin our investigation with Strong's **Greek** concordance **#4521**. *sabbaton sab'-bat-on of Hebrew origin (7676); the Sabbath (i.e. Shabbath),* **or day of weekly repose from secular** *avocations (also the observance or institution itself); by extension.*

I parsed the definitions of individual words for a clearer idea, and the word "repose" means "a state of rest, sleep, or tranquility." In truth, variations of the definition of the Sabbath in Hebrew or Greek aren't indistinguishable at all in accordance with its usage. Any variations came from the Jewish hierarchy, along with their oral laws dictating what was and wasn't proper to do on the Sabbath. The basic definition stays the same in any language, *"a day of rest."*

The Greek version is a derivative of Aramaic or Hebrew, but its meaning, as I have already noted, is the same.

Why else would the Pharisees chastise the Messiah for letting His disciples pluck grain on the Sabbath day?
At that time Jesus was walking through some fields of grain on a Sabbath day. His followers were hungry, so they began to pick the grain and eat it. 2 When the Pharisees saw this, they

said to Jesus, "Look! Your followers are doing what is **unlawful to do on the Sabbath day***."* **(Matthew 12:1-2)**

This becomes important because there is a distinction when regarding **John 19: 31**, which says: *Now then, since it was the* **day of preparation***, to prevent the bodies from remaining on the cross on the Sabbath (for that* **Sabbath was a high day***), the Jews requested of Pilate that their legs be broken, and the bodies be taken away.*

A high day is a New Testament term used to describe one of the annual holy days listed in Leviticus 23, which we already went through. Other than in the book of John, the term "high day" doesn't occur anywhere else in scriptures. Clearly, it's referring to a day of cessation from work because it was a preparation day before a special day important enough to give a distinct sub-title. It doesn't make sense if this preparation day is referencing a weekly Sabbath. If that's the case, why not call it a weekly 7th day or simply, Sabbath instead of a high day if all references of the Sabbath only mean the 7th day?

With Sherlock Holmes and Watson still on the case of the missing Sabbath, we will enlist their aid a bit further in this matter. Scriptures prove the Messiah's death and burial simply could not have been on a Friday preparation day, Shocker, RIGHT? Simple deduction using scriptures eliminates any doubt this is an annual holy day and not the weekly Sabbath. John is very specific about the timing of events, and his statement that this was a preparation day is an important clue.

I went through this exercise in another one of my books, "Unveiling the Sabbath," and it would be an excellent source to study the long version of what I'm about to reveal in the scriptures.

Since it was clear the body of the Messiah had to be removed from the stake because a high Sabbath was quickly approaching. The Hebrew law states a body wasn't to hang on a tree overnight, and touching a dead body would make a person unclean. The last thing any religious Hebrew wanted before an annual or weekly Sabbath was to become unclean or defiled according to the Levitical law. Becoming unclean at that time would exclude any Hebrews from participating in any celebrations until the following day. This would be especially important on an annual high Sabbath that only comes around once a year.

In addition, the exact amount of time Jesus was in the tomb was three days and three nights, according to the Messiah's own words. The Messiah's sign to humanity defies the notion of a Friday afternoon death and burial and an early Sunday morning resurrection? **Matthew 12:38-40**. *"Then some of the scribes and Pharisees said to Him, "Teacher, we want to see a sign from You." 39 But He answered and said to them, "An evil and adulterous generation craves for a sign; and yet no sign will be given to it but the sign of Jonah the prophet; 40 for just as JONAH WAS THREE DAYS AND THREE NIGHTS IN THE BELLY OF THE SEA MONSTER, so will the Son of Man be three days and three nights in the heart of the earth"*

Either the Messiah lied, or there has to be another way of counting days, and since I don't care to insinuate the Messiah lied, our counting of days must be off in determining time. Let's do the honorable thing and listen to the Messiah.

Missed in the entire conversation is the fact the scriptures show two distinct preparation days the week of the Messiah's execution. Remember I said John mentioned this was a preparation day and that fact becomes very important? This adds to the mounting proof the Messiah died on Wednesday afternoon and not Friday. Look a little further, and you'll see the proof unveil itself before your eyes. Take note of the bolded sections of the verses.

Luke 23:55-56, *It was **a preparation day**, and **a Sabbath was about to begin**. 55 Now the women who had come with Him from Galilee followed, and they saw the tomb and how His body was laid. 56 And then **they returned and prepared spices and perfumes**.*

Also, **Mark's 16:1** account, states: *"Now **when the Sabbath was past**, Mary Magdalene, Mary the mother of James, and Salome **bought spices** [which they **could not have purchased on a Sabbath day**], that they might come and anoint Him"*

The women would have been required to wait until this Sabbath was over before they could even buy or begin to prepare spices to be used for anointing Jesus' body.

The worldly scenario goes something like this. Christ was laid in the tomb on Friday at sunset (just before the beginning of the weekly Sabbath) and rose Sunday morning (*after sunrise*). If spices couldn't be bought or prepared until the Sabbath was over, one has to wonder when the women had time to do all this? I have one more wrench to throw into the works.

Luke 23:56 *And **they returned**, and prepared spices and ointments; and **rested the sabbath day** according to the commandment.*

The scriptures tell us when they prepared the spices, and it wasn't after the weekly Sabbath, which would have been the only time available for such a task in the world's scenario.

Clearly, at a minimum, a day elapsed between when they laid the Messiah in the tomb and when the spices were bought and prepared.

If the Messiah had been put to death and sealed within the tomb on Friday before the weekly Sabbath, there would have been no time to buy and prepare spices, which is a lengthy process. Typically, the custom of the Jews was to wash the body (**Acts 9:37**),afterwards, anoint the body by spreading a mixture of aromatics over it, which would slow the decaying process. This was followed by covering the body with a linen winding-sheet while mixing more of the pulverized myrrh and aloes spread into the layers of the linen. The spices were then "*spread over the sheet or bandages in which the body was wrapped*" (**Vincent's Word Studies** comments on **John 19:40**).

The process of grinding down at least one hundred pounds of spices and ointments would have taken several hours, not an easy choir for anyone.

It would have been inconceivable the women would have found a merchant willing to sell the necessary items after sunset on a weekly Sabbath. There was no conceivable way to achieve this spectacular feat.

They first prepared the spices and then **rested on the weekly Sabbath**. When could they do this if the Messiah was laid to rest on a Friday before the Sabbath?

My point in going through this is to show there were two Sabbaths and two preparation days that week. The scriptures bear that out, expressly saying one Sabbath was an annual high Sabbath day. Those that say the term Sabbath is never used in conjunction with an annual holy day are simply wrong and scripture bears that fact out.

That was a high-day, a Sabbath marking the first Day of Unleavened Bread, lasting from Wednesday sunset to Thursday sunset that week.

The Messiah was entombed late in the evening of the 14th or after sundown which was the beginning of the 15th according to His own words. The Messiah would have been resurrected at around the same time, three days and three nights later. He remained in the tomb from Wednesday at sunset until Saturday at sunset, when He rose from the dead.

Why the Word "Sabbath"?

Proverbs 27:17, *As iron sharpens iron,So one person sharpens another.*

William F. Dankenbring

I would like to give credit to a man I never met but whose work has taken on a new meaning these last days; that man was William F. Dankenbring.

I didn't copy his work, I spent time doing my own research before I became aware of his evangelism. I found much the same information as he did and dug up information through many of the same sources and proof text to verify what is accurate. But, one part of his written work, "The Awesome Secret of Counting the Omer to Pentecost!" I came to realize he did a much better job explaining the meaning of the word Sabbath as it translates into the meaning of weeks. So, I'll let him tell you in his own words that meaning.

Quote, "If the counting is to begin the Day after Passover, why didn't the command say, "Begin the day after Passover"?

First of all, that would not have been clear, because people could have thought the 14th Day of Nisan was meant, the Day the Passover lamb was killed! Or, they could have thought the 15th day was meant, the Day the Passover was eaten! Which would have been correct? Confusion would have abounded without further clarification. However, Eliyahu Kitov points out, "The Torah, when referring to Pesach [Passover], uses a different term from that used for the other Festivals, referring to it once as Shabbat but never as Shabbaton. Moreover, it is referred to as Shabbat only in conjunction with the mitzvah of counting the omer, and there the Torah twice refers to the Festival as Shabbat" (page 687). In The Book of Our Heritage by Eliyahu Kitov, Vol. 2, Adar – Nisan, page 691, Joshua 5:11 relates: *"And they ate from the produce of the land from the 'morrow of Pesach* (Passover)'"*. Says Eliyahu Kitov, "The Torah states [Leviticus 23:14], 'you shall not eat bread or parched grain or green grain until this day'[i.e., when the omer is brought]. In the book of Yehoshua [5:11] we find: 'And they ate from the produce of the land from the morrow of Pesach.' [Interestingly, this is the only source in Tanach where the fifteenth of Nisan is referred to as Pesach.].Were you to postpone that Pesach that year fell on a Shabbat as the fools [i.e., the Sadducees conjectured], how is it possible that the permission to eat new grains would be made dependent by the Torah upon something totally unrelated [i.e., the day of the week]—on pure happenstance! Rather, since this [the eating of new grain] was made dependent upon 'the morrow of the Pesach,' it is obvious that 'the morrow of the Pesach' is the reason why new grains are permitted, and we pay no attention to the day of the week" (p.691). The Sadducees had strayed from the fold of Israel during the time of the second Temple. They said that when the Torah said "on the morrow of the Shabbat" it was referring to the day following the weekly Sabbath (Sunday, rather than the Day after the Festival (Passover). Says Eliyahu Kitov, "Our tradition is that [the reference is] not to Sabbath [the day] but to the Festival, and this was seen in the PROPHETS AND THE SANHEDRIN OF EVERY GENERATION who brought the Omer on Nisan 16" (p.691).

Seven "Sabbaths" or Seven "Weeks"?

In **Leviticus 23:15**, where we read we are to count "seven sabbaths" – does it mean literal Sabbath days, or seven weeks?

The Rotherham translation has a footnote at this verse which says: "Seven sabbaths = seven weeks. Compare N.T. (New Testament) Ap. 'Sabbath.'" Turning to the Appendix to the Rotherham New Testament, we find a section on "Sabbath." Rotherham says, "A few critical remarks on the word Sabbath as it appears in the The New Testament may be useful. First, this word seems to be sometimes an appellative [of or relating to a common noun] and sometimes a proper name ('day of rest,' 'Sabbath'). Second, the term Sabbath is, in several texts, used in the plural in the Greek, where, nevertheless, it is evident that only one particular day is intended. Under this head, the following texts are worthy of note: **Mat.12:1, 11; Mark 1:21; 2:23; 3:2; Luke 4:16; 13:10; Acts 13:14.; 16:13**. In all these passages the word in the original is in the plural, and yet it is plain that a particular, individual day is intended. Nor is there anything surprising in this; for 'the Hebrew at times uses plural forms where other languages employ the singular.'"

Rotherham adds, "Third, the word sabbath is extended to signify 'week.' Even in this there is nothing very far fetched; since the transition from the idea of 'rest' to that of a 'rest bounded period of seven days' is a comparatively natural one. Still the question must be considered mainly as one of fact; although, even so, more demonstrative evidence should not be demanded than the nature of the case admits of; and it often suffices to attach a new meaning to a word, that the ordinary application of it is repeatedly seen to be unnatural, illogical, bewildering, or absurd. Hence the current opinion is probably correct that finds notwithstanding that the word for 'week' is here sabbaton in the singular; since it would appear a very paltry boast to say, 'I fast twice on the sabbath' when anyone (with more pleasantry than pharisaism) might reply, 'I fast three times.'"

Rather ridiculous, isn't it? No one would boast about fasting twice in a single day! That would be preposterous! Obviously, the word – as in this case – sometimes means "week," just as translators all have it! Rotherham goes on: "To this example of sabbaton in the singular, used in the sense of 'week,' may now be added **I Corinthians 16:2,** where not only Westcott and Hort, but the entire board of Revisers find the word in the singular number; and it would seem enough simply to ask the question, "Is it credible that the apostle Paul meant to enjoin on the assemblies of Galatia and on that of Corinth to lay by on 'the first [hour] of the sabbath' without so much as specifying that it was the first HOUR of the Day that he intended? If not, and if 'first day of the day' is impossible, what is left but to assume that he meant 'first [day] of the week'? 'Week' also approves itself in **Mat.28:1; Mark 16:2; Luke 24:1; John 20:1, 19; Acts 20:7.** . . There is nothing unnatural in supposing the meaning to be 'week'; for, as we have seen: (a) the word in the plural form may convey a singular idea; (b) the word in the singular is twice used in the sense of 'week.' Now let us test the two words 'sabbaths' and 'week': 'Late in the Sabbaths, as it was on the point of dawning into the first of the Sabbaths.' Will that stand? Now try 'week': 'Late in the week, as it was on the point of dawning into the first of the week.' Here everything is harmonious. With the Hebrews the Sabbath closed the week. Late on the Sabbath would be late in the week, and the transition is natural from the end of one week to the beginning of the next. Hence the correct rendering here is 'week'" (Rotherham Emphasized Bible, Appendix, p.271). How plain can it be? The Greek word sabbaton not only means "Sabbath," but it also clearly means "WEEK"!

I thank the Eternal God for letting me become aware of

men like William F. Dankenbring and others who have discarded the worldview of the Bible and taken on the challenge of finding the truth. They have weathered the storms and their crusades for the truth at a significant cost – segregating them from many friends and family. Rest in Peace and God bless.

Where to Start Counting

1 Timothy 6:10, *For the love of money is a root of all sorts of evil, and some by longing for it have wandered away from the faith and pierced themselves with many griefs.*

    Now that I feel we have securely established the true meaning of the word Sabbath, we might be able to make some additional progress in our investigation.

    Leviticus 23:11 it says, *"He shall wave the sheaf before the Eternal for you to be accepted; on the day after the **Sabbath (1st Day of Unleavened bread)** the priest shall wave it."* The *Lexham English Septuagint*

    As previously stipulated, the word "Sabbath" is the center of all the controversy. If one takes this literally and begins their count of fifty days or seven weeks after the weekly Sabbath, they will always have a Sunday Pentecost. But, if we view this verse as saying to count 50 days or seven weeks after the first day of Unleavened Bread, a special high holy day, we would celebrate the Feast of Weeks on the day on which it falls, whatever that day of the week may be.

    The battle began over the meaning of the Sabbath in this verse long before Christians became involved. There were four major groups of the Jewish sects involved in the discussion or disagreement when the Sanhedrin existed in Jerusalem: the Pharisees, Sadducees, Karaites, and Boethusian, who some claim was the Essenes of that time. That's an argument for another day, but suffice it to say, their influence played a major role in how we view the Feast of Weeks or Pentecost today.

    First off, what does history tell us about the Boethusian sect? Their beginnings are shrouded in obscurity, as is the length of the sect's duration.

They were a Jewish sect that had many similarities with the Sadducees. Both parties were influenced by the aristocracy and denied the soul's immortality and the body's resurrection because, according to them, neither doctrine was mentioned in the Torah. They lived in luxury while ridiculing the piety and self-discipline of the Pharisees, including the Pharisees' strict observance of the laws, both oral and written.

The **Talmud**, considered the authoritative compendium of law, lore, and commentary speaks of the Boethusians in derisive tones. The Midrash (ancient commentary on Hebrew scriptures), is entirely correct in saying that the sects found their followers chiefly among the wealthy of society.

The **Mishnah** and the **Baraita** specifically state that the Boethusians opposed the Pharisees on the matter of the Wave Sheaf offering performed at Passover. It was the Boethusians' position that it must be offered **NOT** on the second feast day (Day after the 1st Day of Unleavened Bread) but on the day after the actual Shabbat of the festival week and should always be celebrated on Sunday 50 days later. The Boethusians' division with the Pharisees was so contentious the Boethusians hired false witnesses to lead the Pharisees astray in their calculations of the new moon.

Other disputes between the Boethusians and Pharisees included whether the high priest should prepare the incense inside or outside the Holy of Holies on Yom Kippur. Whatever their reasonings for these departures from the Temple's normal practices, we'll probably never fully understand. But, we can see; clearly, a hidden agenda caused division between the two.

We know the Messiah told the Sadducees they were ignorant of the laws; did that include the Boethusians since they followed much of the same beliefs? This occurrence was recorded in **Matthew 22:24-29** NASB. *On that Day some*

Sadducees (who say there is no resurrection) came to Jesus and questioned Him, 24 saying, "Teacher, Moses said, 'If a man dies having no children, his brother as next of kin shall marry his wife, and raise up children for his brother.' 25 Now there were seven brothers among us; and the first married and died, and having no children, he left his wife to his brother. 26 It was the same also with the second brother, and the third, down to the seventh. 27 Last of all, the woman died. 28 In the resurrection, therefore, whose wife of the seven will she be? For they all had her in marriage."
*29 But Jesus answered and said to them, **"You are mistaken since you do not understand the Scriptures nor the power of God."***

The Sadducees set a trap for the Messiah using their own logic by asking a question concerning the resurrection, which they claim the Torah denies. What was the Messiah's response? **"You do not understand the scriptures."**

This ignorance of the Torah appears to be backed up by Paul's (a Pharisee) condemnation of the Sadducees in **Acts 23:7-8,** NASB, where he points out their beliefs contradict the teachings of the Messiahs', *7 When he said this, a dissension occurred between the Pharisees and Sadducees, and the assembly was divided. 8 For the Sadducees say that there is no resurrection, nor an angel, nor a spirit, but the Pharisees acknowledge them all.*

This would seem a very odd thing for the Messiah to say to a sect of Jews who appeared to have won the arguments over time concerning calendar issues and sighting the New Moons and when to celebrate the Feast of Weeks.

Josephus tells us that ALL THE MULTITUDE followed the teachings of the Pharisees, especially observance of the wave sheaf offering. *"These have SO GREAT A POWER OVER*

*THE MULTITUDE, that when they say anything against the
king or against the high Priest, they are presently believed"*
(Antiquities, XIII, x, 5).

Today God's churches have appeared to have taken sides
with the Sadducees and Boethusians in these matters, the
winners of the debates over the calendar and when to begin
counting to Pentecost. They have unknowingly mimicked the
doctrines of the Sadducees, Boethusian, and Karaites in setting
times and laws.

Yet, the sect of the Pharisees, the debate's losers, were
regarded as the keepers of the law and temple ceremonies who
observed the regulations according to the Torah.
They taught the resurrection, the existence of angels, and the
Holy Spirit, just as the Torah stipulates.

They also observed the first crescent moon (Waxing
moon) as the beginning of months. As a side note Herbert W.
Armstrong, the founder of the WorldWide Church of God,
wrote an article in 1960 (God's Sacred Calendar) admitting the
official starting of months begins with the sighting of the first
crescent moon. Yet, the WorldWide Church of God, and its
offsprings continue to use the astronomical new moon (dark of
the moon) to set the dates for their holy day celebrations, much
like the Sadducees, Boethusian, and Karaites.

The Pharisees also began counting from the second day
of the Passover season (the day after the 1st Day of Unleavened
Bread) fifty days later or seven weeks to celebrate the harvest
festival of Shavuot, another one of those continuous points of
disagreement.

It's not recorded anywhere that the Messiah said the
Pharisees were ignorant of the law. He did call them a brood of
vipers along with the Sadducees in **Matthew 3:7-9** *NASB. But
when he saw many of the Pharisees and Sadducees coming for*

baptism, he said to them, "You offspring of vipers, who warned you to flee from the wrath to come? 8 Therefore produce fruit consistent with repentance; 9 and do not assume that you can say to yourselves, 'We have Abraham as our father'; for I tell you that God is able, from these stones, to raise up children for Abraham

In fact, the Messiah said just the opposite of the Pharisees, **Matthew 23:1-3,** NASB. T*hen Jesus spoke to the crowds and to His disciples, 2 saying: "The scribes and the Pharisees have seated themselves in the chair of Moses. 3 Therefore, whatever they tell you, do and comply with it all, but do not do as they do; for they say things and do not do them.*

He told both the Pharisees and Scribes to repent; both were failing the people in their own special ways. But, keeping the laws according to the Torah wasn't the Pharisee's failing; all the extra burdens they were applying to the laws in oral traditions were the issue.

The Scribes mentioned here were the lawyers within the Hebrew society, whose primary job was to copy and interpret the Scriptures. Their focus became the details or the letter of the law. They transitioned from mere copyists to teachers of the Scriptures, but they were not the Sadducees, as some may claim.

Even though the Messiah claims the Scribes and Pharisees are sitting in Moses' judgment seats, He didn't deny their role in running the Temple. To be clear, He also didn't view their actions as righteous.

The Messiah didn't contradict the Pharisees on the Torah as He did the Sadducees, causing me to wonder who had the correct interpretation of scripture after all? We'll look at the proof text used to back the claims of the different sects a bit later, but first, let's look at our remaining group of Jews.

We haven't spoken about the Karaites and their beliefs, so let's do that now. The Jewish Karaites weren't an official sect until they established roots in Babylonia and Persia in the 8th century CE and late in the 9th century CE within Israel and the middle east.

The Karaites consider the Tanakh as the sole source of religious authority and reject the oral traditions of the Rabbis. Encyclopedia Britannica defines the *Tanakh as an acronym derived from the names of the three divisions of the Hebrew Bible: Torah (Instruction, or Law, also called the Pentateuch), Nevi'im (Prophets), and Ketuvim (Writings). as elaborated by the rabbis in the Mishnah, Talmud, and later halakhic literature.*

When the Karaite movement first coalesced, it threatened rabbinic dominance in the Jewish culture. Their efforts to define doctrine eventually suffered a major pushback by the Jewish community of Rabbis, ending the Karaites' effort to dominate the direction of Jewish teachings.

When studying the Torah's (First Five books of the Hebrew Bible) Karaites endeavored to adhere to the plain or most obvious meaning of the text. One note mentioned it wasn't necessarily always that the literal meaning but rather the meaning that they felt would have been naturally understood by the ancient Hebrews. This interpretation was guided by the principle of their interpretation without the use of the Oral Torah (*legal interpretations that were not recorded in the Five Books of Moses*).

By contrast, Rabbinic Judaism relies on the legal rulings of the Sanhedrin as they are codified in the Midrash, Talmud, and other sources to indicate the authentic meaning of the Torah.

According to Mordecai ben Nissan, the ancestors of the Karaites, emerged from a group called Benei Ṣedeq, which was around during the Second Temple of Herod. One of the debates between Historians concerning Karaism is whether there is a direct connection to the Sadducees. At the end of the Temple (70 CE) Karaism represented several similar views with the Sadducees, just like the Boethusians.

Karaites today don't deny the similarities to the Sadducees due mainly to the rejection of rabbinical authority and the oral law. They also see the Sadducees' interpretations of the calendar and issues concerning the Feast of Weeks and when to begin counting the same.

Another clue as to why the Karaites side with the Sadducees and Boethusian comes from Karaite scholars known to have been associated with the Tiberian Masoretic tradition around the tenth and eleventh centuries CE. This applies to the Karaite grammarians who were active in Jerusalem towards the end of the Masoretic period.

Comparing the Masoretic discipline of Karaite grammar to core Masoretic activities, scholars are able to identify the authors of some of the Masoretic treatises at the end of the Masoretic period in the 11th century as Karaite.

Several modern scholars have argued that some of the Masoretes themselves were Karaites, in particular Aharon ben Asher, who was one of the most prominent Masoretes towards the end of the Masoretic period in the 10th century. One scholar even suggested that all the Masoretes should be 'suspected' of being Karaites since they spent their time occupied with vocalization and accents of the Bible, and there is no evidence that they showed any interest in the Talmud. In fact, I, too, have been accused of adhering strictly to the Talmud because of my beliefs concerning Shavuot or the Feast of Weeks.

Wikipedias' definition of the Talmud is the central text of Rabbinic Judaism and the primary source of Jewish religious law (halakha) and Jewish theology. Until the advent of modernity, in nearly all Jewish communities, the Talmud was the centerpiece of Jewish cultural life and was foundational to "all Jewish thought and aspirations," also serving as "the guide for the daily life" of Jews.

Whoever these folks were, and still are, the debate is ongoing. They appear to be more interested in opposing the established teachings than finding the truth.

This concludes the description of the trio of nemesis against the Pharisees, who are opposed to many different doctrines. But what was the source of their information causing the contentious atmosphere?

Concerning the Sadducees, the other major sect of the Jews, which included some of the aristocracy and some of the high priests, who counted Pentecost from the day after the weekly Sabbath which fell during the Days of Unleavened Bread, Josephus tells us: "*. . . the Sadducees are able to persuade NONE BUT THE RICH, and have not the populous obsequious to them, but the Pharisees have the MULTITUDE ON THEIR SIDE. . .*" (Anti., XIII, x, 6).

Leaders of churches have a way of finding a version of truth bought and paid for by those controlling the purse strings. Money was the root of evil, feeding the controversies between these groups.

I'm not a fan of the Pharisees by the smallest measure, but they kept the laws and oracles according to Paul. **Romans 3:2,** *Great in every respect. First, that they were entrusted with the actual words of God.*

They observed those oracles we have forgotten and have become hidden from the minds of modern-day believers. First, the Babylonians, then the Greeks and finally, the Romans did all they could through different sects of the Jews to influence the change of God's word to reflect more to their own.

At the beginning, it was through coercion, intimidation, and lots of money over hundreds of years that created the divide in thought. Once enough time elapsed, these things became the norm and became traditions that have taken hold. What else has the pagan world bought and hidden that belongs to God?

Translations

Galatians 1:8, *But even if we, or an angel from heaven, should preach to you a gospel contrary to what we have preached to you, he is to be accursed!*

The expression "Death by a thousand cuts" originated in Imperial China around 900 CE as torture, resulting in the execution of a prisoner. Death by a thousand cuts carries the literal meaning, one small cut may not be harmful, but a thousand small cuts will kill a person. One can see this torturous practice playing out in a biblical sense while trying to apply the correct meaning to a verse, particularly...**Leviticus 23:11.**

Modern Day advocates of counting from the weekly Sabbath apply the ancient method of silencing and dicing dissenters with their doctrine of a thousand modern translations. They insist on a literal translation of the word Sabbath in **Leviticus 23:11**. Denying its correct translation as Holy day, Passover, or 1st Day of Unleavened Bread.

Did the meaning of the word Sabbath change in one drastic revelation? And, did the new doctrine actually take hundreds or thousands of years to creep into scripture before the deception was complete?

Other less objectionable doctrines often go unnoticed or unchallenged in Churchianity until it's too late. Those who view the Sabbath as a weekly or annual holy day are told the debate is over; the word Sabbath can only mean the weekly Sabbath. Sit down and stop rocking the boat or get out, or we'll honor our god by shutting you up.

Ignoring those voices and in my zeal to find the truth, I figuratively traveled back in time to find the correct meaning of **Leviticus 23:11**. Since little in the way of written biblical evidence is available prior to 300 BCE, it requires us to first avail ourselves of the best and oldest known sources.

First, let me say when quoting from scripture or from any historians, there is always someone who will ridicule one or more of the authors or translations. I'll be blunt, I don't care how one feels or thinks about translations or sources; any legitimate source is evidence of the attitudes and thinking of the men and women eons ago, and that's highly relevant to finding the truth.

Each time I look backwards in time to the era before Christ, I am able to find more information to support my assertions. In my amateur but extensive research, I have found blaring contradictions to modern translations of **Leviticus 23:11** from several older known sources. So, criticizing one source or proof text may gain traction in modern churches, but the task of defending one's position remains relevant because there are more than just one or two sources.

The number one source on my list is the Greek Septuagint. from the Latin: Septuagint, meaning 'seventy'; often abbreviated 70; in Roman numerals, LXX. It is the earliest Greek translation of books from the Hebrew Bible into another language.

It is the oldest and most complete translation of the Hebrew Bible made by the Jews in existence today. Without the Septuagint, we would be ignorant of many of the ancient truths sending us wandering in darkness.

The first five books of the Hebrew Bible, known as the Torah or the Pentateuch, were part of the original Septuagint some 2300 years ago. Hebrew was translated to the Greek language in the mid-3rd century BCE because of the influence the Alexandrian Greeks inserted upon that region of the world.

The Lexham English translation of the Septuagint supports a yearly annual Sabbath definition of **Leviticus 23:11**. Look at how it describes the wave sheaf. *Verse 11, And he will offer up the sheaf in the presence of the Eternal, acceptable on your behalf. <u>On the next day **after the first**</u>, the Priest will offer it up.*

This translation by itself wouldn't be the smoking gun to convince many nay-sayers. But the Septuagint is supported by the Targums. What is Targum, you ask? Let me quote the **Encyclopedia Britannica**: *"Some of the first translations of the Torah began during the Babylonian exile when Aramaic became the main language of the Jews. With most people speaking only Aramaic and not understanding Hebrew, the Targum were created to allow the common person to understand the Torah as it was read in ancient synagogues."*

The Hebrew Bible, specifically the Torah, was translated into Aramaic, which was created around the same time as the later Septuigents 1st and 2nd century BCE.
So, how does the Targum convey the passage in question?

Here is **Leviticus 23:11,** *and he shall uplift the sheaf before the Eternal to be accepted for you. After the **first festal Day of Pascha** (or, the Day after the feast-day of Pascha) on the day on which you elevate the sheaf,*

The Targum seems straightforward enough, but that still isn't enough proof for those teetering on the edge of indecisiveness.

An additional translation to consider is the Hebrew Tanakh called the Chabad translation. **Leviticus 23:11,** *And he shall wave the omer before the Eternal so that it will be acceptable for you; the kohen shall wave it on the day **after the rest day**.*

Rabbi Rashi Commentary on the day after the rest day: מִמָּחֳרַת הַשַּׁבָּת. On the day after the first holy Day of Passover, [since a holy festival day is also שַׁבָּת, rest day, in scripture]. For if you say [that it means] the "Sabbath of Creation" [i.e., the actual Sabbath, the seventh day of the week], you would not know which one. - [Men. 66a]

This also goes back to the idea that Sabbath can only mean the 7th day of the week, and we have already seen where that isn't always the case.

In light of 3 out of 4 major sects practicing in the Jewish religions today, and interpreting this verse describing an annual Sabbath and NOT the weekly Sabbath, overwhelming evidence concludes this is the 1st Day of Unleavened Bread. It's true; the modern Karaite movement is one modern Jewish sect that doesn't see this as an annual holy day. Who would have guessed these folks would oppose the teachings handed down from prior centuries.

A few modern Bibles use the translations from the Septuagint and Targum as their bases of understanding. The translation called "Names of God Bible" does so in a very straight and understandable fashion.

Leviticus 23:10 NOG *"Tell the Israelites: When you come to the land I am going to give you and you harvest grain, bring the Priest a bundle of the first grain you harvest. 11 He will present it to Yahweh so that you will be accepted. He will present it on the **Day after Passover.***

In addition to this NOG translation, there is the Wycliffe Bible Commentary that quotes the same passage in this way. *11 and the Priest shall raise up a bundle before the Eternal, that it be acceptable for you, in the together Day of the Sabbath, that is, **of (the) pask**; and the Priest shall hallow that bundle; (and the Priest shall raise up, or shall wave, the sheaf* *as a special gift before the Eternal, so that you gain acceptance; yea, on the day after the Sabbath, that is, **the day after the Passover**, the Priest shall dedicate that sheaf;)*

The **Wycliff commentary** goes on to say the word Sabbath is the 1st Day of Unleavened Bread because the definition of Sabbath simply means to "cease, to rest, to come to an end."

Who was John Wycliff?

This is one intro to the Wycliff bible, *"Throughout medieval times the English church was governed from Rome by the Pope. All over the Christian world, church services were conducted in Latin. It was illegal to translate the Bible into local languages. John Wycliffe was an Oxford professor who believed that the teachings of the Bible were more important than the earthly clergy and the Pope. Wycliffe translated the Bible into English, as he believed that everyone should be able to understand it directly.*

Wycliffe inspired the first complete English translation of the Bible, and the Lollards, who took his views in extreme forms, added to the Wycliffe Bible commentaries such as this one in Middle English. Made probably just before Henry IV issued the first orders for burnings to punish heretics in 1401, this manuscript escaped a similar fate.

Wycliffe was too well connected and lucky to have been executed for heresy, although the archbishop of Canterbury condemned him. The support of his Oxford colleagues and influential layman, as well as the anti-clerical leanings of King Richard II, who resisted ordering the burning of heretics, saved his life. Forty years after his death, the climate had changed, and his body was dug up, and along with his books, were burned and scattered. Nonetheless, the English translations had a lasting influence on the language."

Another final commentary on the man and the Wycliffe Bible. The Bible and commentary were edited by 48 different biblical scholars representing a wide section of American protestant Christianity. It also said these same scholars examined the entire biblical text **phrase by phrase.**

I must say, I'm mystified, given the history of this work and as to why protestants in mass claim the opposite must be true of what these men say and the meaning behind **Leviticus 23:11**.

Perhaps this is one of the reasons Wycliff was dug up 40 years after his death and his bones burned. Revealing the truth can bring the worst out of some believers.

Flavius Josephus was a noted Jewish historian of the first century, a priest, a famous general in the war against the Romans in 70 A.D., **and a Pharisee**. He writes about the celebration of Pentecost: *"**On the second day of unleavened bread**, that is to say the **sixteenth**, our people partake of the crops which they have reaped and which have not been touched till then, and esteeming it right first to do homage to God, to whom they owe the abundance of these gifts, they offer to him the first-fruits of the barley in the following way. After parching and crushing the little sheaf of ears and purifying the barley for grinding, they bring to the altar an as'saron [ie, omer] for God, and, having flung a handful thereof on the altar, they leave the rest for the use of the priests. Thereafter all are permitted, publicly or individually, to begin harvest."*

Josephus, Antiquities 3.250-251, in Josephus IV Jewish Antiquities Books I-IV, Loeb Classical Library, Harvard University Press, Cambridge, 1930, pp. 437-439.

Another contemporary historian Philo, writing the following THE SIXTH FESTIVAL, XXIX. (162) *"There is also a **festival on the day of the paschal feast**, which **succeeds the first day**, and **this is named the sheaf**, from what takes place on it; for the sheaf is brought to the altar as a first fruit both of the country which the nation has received for its own, and also of the whole land; so as to be an offering both for the nation separately, and also a common one for the whole race of mankind; and so that the people by it worship the living God, both for themselves and for all the rest of mankind, because they have received the fertile earth for their inheritance; for in the country there is no barren soil, but even all those parts which appear to be stony and rugged are surrounded with soft veins of great depth, which, by reason of their richness, are very well suited for the production of living things."*

The noted Biblical commentary C.F. Keil, D.D. and F. Delitzsch, D.D.in Vol. One of the Pentateuch said the following. *"When the Israelites had come into the land to be given them by the Eternal and has reaped the harvest, they were to bring a sheaf as first-fruits of their harvest to the priest, that he might wave it before Jehovah on the day after the Sabbath, i.e., after the first day of Mazzoth. . . . "(the morrow after the Sabbath) signifies the next day after the **first day of the feast of Mazzoth**, i.e., the **16th Abib (Nisan)**, **not the day of the Sabbath** which fell in the seven days' feast of Mazzoth, as the Baethoseans supposed, still less the 22nd of Nisan, or the day after the conclusion of the seven days' feast . . ."* (volume 1, p.613).

The commentary continues to elaborate as to the correct day in which we must begin counting. *"The 'Sabbath' does not mean the seventh day of the week, but the day of rest, although the weekly Sabbath was always the seventh or last day of the*

week; hence not only the seventh day of the week (Exo.31:15, etc.), but the day of atonement (the tenth of the seventh month) is called 'Sabbath,' and Shabbath shabbathon' (v. 32 , ch.16:31). As a day of rest, on which no laborious work was to be performed (v.8), the first Day of the Feast of Mazzoth is called 'Sabbath,' irrespectively of the day of the week upon which it fell; and 'the morrow after the Sabbath' is equivalent to 'the morrow after the Passover' mentioned in Joshua 5:11, where 'Passover' signifies the day at the beginning of which the paschal meal was held, i.e., the first day of unleavened bread, which commenced on the evening of the 14th, in other words, the 15th Abib"
(p.614).

Who's right and who's wrong? We can stand on tradition and be adamant we are correct, or we can pray we are celebrating the Feast of Weeks on the correct day as the majority of Jews. God expects us to be celebrating when He is celebrating not the day before or the day after, but on the same day.

Regardless of what we feel in our hearts, it's essential we try and get it right. Isn't that in itself enough reason to further investigate our positions in these matters?

The Temple
By Alfred Edersheim
And
Unger Bible Dictionary

2 Corinthians 13:1, *This is the third time that I am coming to you. On the testimony of two or three witnesses every matter shall be confirmed.*

I include these two together since they both give a similar narrative of the Feast of Weeks. The works of Alfred Edersheim of the life and times within the Temple Ministry are works referenced many times in theological circles. He is considered one of the leading authorities regarding the doctrines and practices of Judaism, offers this view, The Expression, *"the morrow after the Sabbath" (lev. 23:11), has sometimes been misunderstood as implying that the presentation of the so-called "First sheaf," was to be always made on the day following the weekly Sabbath of the Passover week. This view was adopted by the "Boethusians" and the Sadducees in the time of Christ and by the Karaite Jews and certain modern interpreters rest on a misunderstanding of the word "sabbath"* **(Leviticus 23:24, 32, 39)**.

"As in analogous allusions to other feasts in the same chapter, it means not the weekly Sabbath, but the day of the festival. The testimony of Josephus (antiq. 3.248-249), of (Philo (Op. ii. 294), and Jewish tradition leaves no room to doubt that in this instance, we are to understand by the "Sabbath" the 15th of Nisan, on whatever day of the week it might fall."

Unger's Bible Commentary also makes the same point: the wave sheaf was presented on the 1st Day of the Feast of Unleavened Bread, and the count began on the 2nd day of

Unleavened Bread toward the celebration of the Feast of Weeks.

The following were the offerings to be waved before the Eternal—the breast of a private thank offering (**Leviticus 7:30**); the fat, breast, and shoulder of the thank offerings at the consecration of the priests, the so-called consecration of offerings (**Exodus 9:22–26; Leviticus 8:25–29**); the firstling sheaf offered on the 2nd Day of Unleavened Bread (**Leviticus 23:11**);

Symbolic Meanings

Jeremiah 10:2, *Thus says the Lord: "Learn not the way of the nations, nor be dismayed at the signs of the heavens because the nations are dismayed at them,*

There is this nagging question of the symbolism regarding the Messiah and His miraculous meeting with Mary in the garden the morning after His resurrection. At this meeting, He informed Mary not to touch Him because He had not yet ascended to the Father in heaven. I have no argument with the fact they met together, and events unfolded as stated in scripture. This event is supported by the testimony of the disciples, and the Messiah told Mary He had not yet ascended to the Father in heaven.

The prestigious churches of God have taught for decades; the meeting with Mary was prior to the wave sheaf (Messiah) being symbolically offered up as the sacrifice of first fruits. Nowhere in scriptures does it say this event was when the wave sheaf was offered.

In my and others' opinions, this is purely supposition that involves procedural issues that don't ceremonially allow for a wave sheaf offering three days after the Messiah's death. Had that been the case, why wasn't the wave sheaf offered the next morning after the Messiah's death when the actual wave sheaf would have been presented at the Temple as protocol demands?

The wave sheaf was cut after sunset on the eve of the 15th (which is the beginning of the 16th), then offered the next morning (still the 16th) by the Priest in the Temple. They never waited three days and nights before presenting Omar before God. Let me stipulate here that offering putrefied rotting flesh to the Eternal is an abomination. At no time would the Priest kill an animal and wait three days before performing the rest of the necessary rites.

Here is the accounting of the exact cutting of the wave sheaf in Israel while the systems were still in place. The accounting is from Alfred Edersheim's *"The Temple. Already on the 14th of Nisan, the spot whence the first sheaf was to be reaped had been marked out by delegates from the Sanhedrin by tying together in bundles, while still standing, the barley that was to be cut down. Though for obvious reasons, it was customary to choose for this purpose the sheltered Ashes-valley across Kedron, there was no restriction on that point, provided the barley had grown in an ordinary field–of course in Palestine itself–and not in garden or orchard land, and that the soil had not been manured nor yet artificially watered. When the time for cutting the sheaf had arrived, that is, on the evening of the 15th of Nisan (even though it were the Sabbath), just as the sun went down, three men, each with a sickle and basket, formally set to work. But in order clearly, to bring out all that was distinctive in the ceremony, they first asked the bystanders three times each of these questions: Has the sun gone down? With this sickle? Into this basket? On this Sabbath (or the First Pass-over day)? And lastly, Shall I reap? Having each time been answered in the affirmative, they cut down barley to the amount of one ephah, or ten omers, or three seahs, which is equal to about three pecks and three pints of our English measure. The ears were brought into the court of the Temple, and thrashed out with canes or stalks so as not to injure the corn; then parched on a pan perforated with holes so that each grain might be touched by the fire, and finally exposed to the wind."*

I think Unger's Bible Dictionary describes the same events as Alfred Edersheim but is more in sync with the New Testament timeline.

Let me try and break this down for you because if it's symbolism you want, then symbolism you'll get. The wave sheaf was more important than we ever realized, and the story needs to be told, so God's people have all the information.

On the morning of the 14th of Abib/Aviv, delegates from the Sanhedrin made a short journey over the Kedron valley to select the field where the wave sheaf would be cut. Once selected, they marked out a spot bundling together three groups of stalks with the desired amount of grain while still standing. These three bundles were calculated to reap three omers of grain.

As stated by Edersheim, this was barley grown in the sheltered Ashes Valley across the Kedron, where there was no restriction except the barley had to be grown in Palestine without being fertilized by manure or artificially watered. This was an essential element because one bundle did represent the Messiah.

Ironically, this was most likely occurring around the same time the Messiah was being examined by the Priest and later on by Pilate prior to His lifting up on the stake.

We know this because of what John reported about the Priest. **John 18:28**, *Then they brought Jesus from Caiaphas into the Praetorium, and it was early; and they themselves did not enter the Praetorium, so that they would not be defiled, but might eat the Passover.*

Being the ever so righteous Priest, they do not want to dirty their hands or be seen being defiled before such a momentous annual event. This occurred before the 9 o'clock hour, the first offering of morning Temple sacrifices, and the time the Messiah was hoisted up as reported in the scriptures. It's also interesting that the Messiah was executed with two other men, making the total count…three, corresponding to the three bundles of barley waiting to be harvested.

Without getting too much further into details about the events of the Messiah's death, we know the timeline was occurring on the 14th of Aviv/Abib because it was the preparation day before the 1st Day of Unleavened Bread. Torah restrictions prohibit bodies to remain upon the cross past sundown and into the High Sabbath day" **John 19:31**, *Now then, since it was the day of preparation, to prevent the bodies from remaining on the cross on the Sabbath (for that Sabbath was a high day), the Jews requested of Pilate that their legs be broken, and the bodies be taken away*

The Messiah must die and be placed in the tomb before or at sunset—before the beginning of the High day celebrations, the 1st Day of Unleavened Bread.
(Sanhedrin, Mishnah IV.1; cf. **Deuteronomy 21:23** ref. *"His body shall not remain all night upon the tree"*.

It's commonly believed the Messiah took his last breath around 3 PM at the exact moment the Temple priest slew the Passover Lamb.

According to Josephus, this could have been "from the ninth hour till the eleventh" (3 PM to 5 PM) (The Jewish War, VI.9.3).

Whether it was 3 PM or 5 PM, there was this rush to remove the Messiah's body from His execution pole and prepare a hasty burial in the tomb of Joseph of Arimathea.

We also know it probably took some time to claim the body and hastily prepare it with available ointments and herbs.

Here is where it gets interesting because, according to Unger's and Edersheim, on the evening of the 15th the High day a procession of people and Priests made their way down the Kidron valley to where the bundles of barley wheat awaited.

The evening before, several different events were in the process of happening all at once all around Jerusalem at this time. Slaughtered lambs were being roasted in preparation for the Passover meal on the evening of the 14th, the wave sheaf was waiting to be cut while the Messiah was being murdered and buried.

As the sun went down on the 15th, three men stood ready with sickles to harvest the first fruits of the barley. As a side note, it didn't dawn on me that the evening of the 15th sunset was the beginning of the 16th. We in this western world have been programmed to think the day ends at midnight, but that isn't how God calculates a day. The day ends and begins when the sun is set according to God's calculations.

The darkness is always before light (**Genesis 1:2-3**). Afterward, God brings "light" to the world as the morning sun and defines it as a morning: "And there was evening, and there was morning, the first day." This is repeated several times over in the following passages of **Genesis (1:8; 1:13; 1:19; 1:23; 1:31).** This is the basic pattern as God created the first 7 days and is from sundown to sundown.

It's also repeated in Yom Kippur—the "day" of atonement—from evening to evening (**Leviticus 23:32**).

Now, back to the incredible events of that 15th and 16th as they unfolded. As the 15th came to a close with the setting of the sun. The Messiah was already unquestionably in the tomb for approximately 24 hours, and the stone door was securely sealed shut.

At the same time the sun was dipping under the horizon, the first fruit harvest began. A small contingent of folks stood around the reapers as they took their positions in preparation for cutting the ceremonial harvest.

The reapers began asking the crowd a series of questions three different times while garnering a repetitious response.
Has the sun gone down? Their reply must be, Yes!
The high Sabbath (1st day of Unleavened bread) was over and the sun was down below the horizon.
With this sickle? Once again, Yes!
Into this basket? And, Yes!
And lastly, Shall I reap? A resounding yes! Which would have echoed out across the valley.

With a swift and accurate thrust, the sickles cut through the stalks loosening from their roots. These were the first of the first fruits to be harvested. Before this evening and the end of that High day, no prior harvesting could occur. Once the first fruits were taken, the next 49 days, all wheat and barley harvest should be completed before celebrating the Feast of Weeks (Shavuot.) The Wave Sheaf, seen as representing the Messiah, happened on the day we are to begin counting to the next First Fruit offering. This makes more sense than saying it was three days later in my estimations.

This is all ironic, considering many of the same people who a day earlier condemned the Messiah were perhaps the voices mixed in with those in the harvest procession.

Once the sun had completely set below the horizon and out of sight on the 15th, counting the omer and Wave Sheaf officially began. Once the sheaves were cut and given to the Priest, the preparation of the barley was to begin for the next morning's presentation in the Temple.

The 15th of Nisan or Aviv/Abib and the Passover meal wasn't just an important yearly event but was essential for every Israelite to participate in, young, old, rich, or poor.

Stop and think about this for a moment; the Messiah's physical life had come to a ghastly and abrupt end just hours earlier as an offering to the Father for the sins of mankind. His human form had ceased to be; only the shell of humanity remained as a witness to His existence.

It's reminiscent of 1400 years earlier before the Israelites crossed into Jordan. The manna that sustained the children of Israel in the wilderness for forty years came to an abrupt end the same day after the 1st Day of Unleavened Bread. They were then commanded to begin eating the New grain being harvested across the Jordan on the morrow after the High Sabbath (1st Day of Unleavened bread).

Joshua 5 draws a picture of that event before Israel crossed the Jordan and God halted the manna. The Darby Translation. **Joshua 5:10-12**, *And the children of Israel encamped in Gilgal, and held the passover on the fourteenth day of the month, at even, in the plains of Jericho. 11. And they ate of the old corn of the land on the morrow after the passover, unleavened loaves, and roasted [corn] on that same day. 12. And the manna ceased on the morrow, when they had eaten of the old corn of the land; and there was no more manna for the children of Israel; and they ate of the produce of the land of Canaan that year.*

Manna, the children of Israel, ate for 40 years in the wilderness suddenly ceased, and they began eating food supplied naturally by the lands in the process of being harvested. Folks have asked, "who planted the barley or wheat the children of Israel began eating?"

The answer is staring us right in the face; the Canaanites planted barley and wheat to be sown for their food source. What was the first thing Israel did after they entered the promised land? They destroyed the city of Jericho along with the inhabitants. The fields of wheat and barley were there for the taking.

John 6:35, Jesus said to them, *"I am the bread of life; the one who comes to Me will not be hungry, and the one who believes in Me will never be thirsty. 36. But I said to you that you have indeed seen Me, and yet you do not believe.*

The Messiah taught His disciples. He was the manna teaching the children of Israel about the Sabbath and His laws that had been corrupted by the world. He has also become the test figure for mankind, just as manna became the test for the children of Israel. When he says I have not come to destroy the laws, do we believe that statement is true?

Matthew 5:17-20, **NASB** *"Do not presume that I came to abolish the Law or the Prophets; I did not come to abolish, but to fulfill. 18. For truly I say to you, until heaven and earth pass away, not the smallest letter or stroke of a letter shall pass from the law, until all is accomplished! 19. Therefore, whoever nullifies one of the least of these commandments, and teaches others to do the same, shall be called least in the kingdom of heaven; but whoever keeps and teaches them, he shall be called great in the kingdom of heaven.*

And here is a twist, when all things are considered, is this statement a reformation of the Pharisees and not so much a put-down?

20. "For I say to you that unless your righteousness far surpasses that of the scribes and Pharisees, you will not enter the kingdom of heaven.

It's interesting that the Messiah ended the statement saying our righteousness must exceed the righteousness of Pharisees and Scribes. In my humble opinion, this is more evidence the Pharisees and scribes were following the written laws, but their sin was adding to the word of God.

Unless we do more to follow those correctly teaching the laws of God, neither can we enter the Kingdom of heaven. **Deuteronomy 4:2,** *You shall not add to the word which I am commanding you, nor take away from it, so that you may keep the commandments of the Eternal your God which I am commanding you.*

Also found in **Revelation 22:18-19** ref.

As further evidence of the corruptness of God's laws, one only needs to ask, Why weren't the Sadducees included in this statement?

Let me indulge myself for just a moment concerning this idea that the Sadducees were lacking in knowledge according to the Messiah. In **Matthew 9: 35** *Jesus was going through all the cities and villages, teaching in their synagogues and proclaiming the gospel of the kingdom, and healing every disease and every sickness.*

Here's my question, "if the teachers of the Torah were doing their jobs correctly, why was it essential for the Messiah to travel about teaching?" We know from the letters of the disciples, He was teaching from the Torah and prophets because it says as much in **Luke 24:44, Matthew 15:7, and Matthew 5:17,** just to name a few instances. So, what was He teaching that was controversial or different?

Perhaps He wasn't teaching contrary to the Torah, but instead, correcting wrong assumptions made by factions of the Jewish sects. Could that be why some accepted his teachings and others were prepared to stone Him?

Okay, I'm done with my indulgence; back to the book.

Since it was a new harvest offering, there was to be no leaven, hence the 1st Day of Unleavened Bread. It represented living in the kingdom with the Messiah in an unleavened state

— a sinless form. For the 7 days of Unleavened Bread is the number of *"fullness"* or *"completeness."*

But there is more to the story because the offering wasn't simply handed off to the Priest marking the end of the Wave Sheaf offering. The grains of the first fruit were then brought to the Temple court. They separated the grain from the stalks with canes so as not to damage the grain...it was essential they stayed whole.

I see this as a stark reminder of the Messiah's body being beaten but not broken. The whole grain was wholly parched by fire within a perforated bowel, so every grain would be individually touched by fire. Every part of the Messiah's body suffered the torment of pain and death.

The grain kernels were then ground and sifted to a required fineness which was ascertained by a (Gizbarim) or treasurer of the Temple.

After the tedious process was completed, three omers of barley flour were parched, sifted, and roasted; then, one omer was separated for the wave sheaf offering in the Temple service.

Any excess remaining flour was redeemed and could be used for any purpose outside the offering. The omer (approx. 14 cups) was mixed with a log (slightly more than 0.5 liters (0.14 U.S. gallon), of oil and a handful of frankincense.

Also, another year-old lamb was sacrificed, along with one quart of wine were offered, all the symbols representing the Messiah.

Once prepared, an omer of barley grain was offered on the morning of the 16th, with the morning sacrifices at the 3rd hour or 9AM.

That evening of the 15th was the beginning of the 16th began the count of seven weeks or Sabbaths to arrive fifty days later for the celebration of Shavuot. The day the wave sheaf was offered was on the 16th of Aviv/Abib, and would have been on a Friday, the day after the high Day of the 1st Day of Unleavened Bread, because it says, on the morrow after the 1st-Day of Unleavened Bread when the count was to began.

Fifty days later in the year, after the Messiah's death and counting from the 2nd day of Passover, you land upon a Friday for the Shavuot or (Feast of Weeks), which is the next harvest festival. If that is the case, **Acts 2:1** NASB states, *"1. When the Day of Pentecost had come, they were all together in one place."* This was not a Sunday but was on a Friday that year.

Sunday, it seems, is a popular day even for God's people, it appears as though we can't get away from making that day a special celebration. I had one gentleman say to me, "Sunday is just another day God created so if Pentecost falls on Sunday, does that make it automatically wrong?" If the day by calculating falls on Sunday, the 1st day of the week, and counting from the day after the 1st Day of Unleavened Bread on the 16th, then the answer is NO! It makes no difference what day of the week the Feast of weeks falls on as long as one begins counting from the 16th. But to purposely engineer the facts to have one of God's High Sabbaths fall on the day pagans venerate to the sun god is an abomination.

The Feast of Weeks isn't a fixed date on the calendar. By making it happen on the same day every year that is not following the will of the One who gave us the Holy days (my opinion).

One last thing before I depart from this portion of the book. Nowhere in the New or Old Testament does it specifically say Pentecost should fall on the 1st day of the week. Only by calculating from the weekly Sabbath within the days of

Unleavened Bread will Pentecost occur every year on a Sunday the 1st day of the week.

But, counting from the 7th day weekly Sabbath that falls within the days of Unleavened bread contradicts the instructions given to Moses by the Eternal. In **Leviticus 23:6** we are told the following, in verse 6, *Then on the fifteenth day of the same month there is the Feast of Unleavened Bread to the Lord; for seven days you shall eat unleavened bread.* Also, **Deuteronomy 16:4** says, *For seven days no leaven shall be seen with you in your entire territory, and none of the meat which you sacrifice on the evening of the first day shall be left overnight until the morning.*

Seems straightforward enough, now, read further down, beginning in **Leviticus 23:14**, *Until this very day, until you have brought in the offering of your God, you shall eat neither bread nor roasted grain nor new produce. It is to be a permanent statute throughout your generations in all your dwelling places.*

Verse says we're to Eat Unleavened Bread everyday (7 days) beginning with the 1st day of Unleavened Bread. Yet, verse 14 says you can't eat any bread or grains before you offer the Wave Sheaf offering to God. What happens if the 1st day of Unleavened Bread falls on a Monday? You must according to verse 14 of Leviticus 23 not eat ANY kind of bread or grains until that following Sunday. Five days would have to pass before you can even eat Unleavened Bread which is commanded we do every day according to verse 6. Which is it, to eat or not to eat? Both cannot be right if we begin counting from the 7th day of the weekly Sabbath.

On the other hand, it makes all the sense in the world if the Wave Sheaf occurs on the Day after the 1st day of Unleavened Bread, (the 16th) one can fulfill both requirements stipulated in this chapter. It's a conundrum for the Pentecost advocate and the answer I am eager to hear.

The same ordinance mentioned in verse 6 of Lev. 23 is first given in **Exodus 12:15-16,** *Seven days you shall eat* ***unleavened bread.*** *On the* ***first day you shall put away leaven out of your houses,*** *for whoever eats leavened bread from the first day until the seventh day, that person shall be cut off from Israel. 16. On the first day there shall be a holy convocation, and on the seventh day there shall be a holy convocation for you. No manner of work shall be done on them; but that which every man must eat—that only may be prepared for you.*

There is one problem we must deal with concerning both these ordinances, one says to eat Unleavened bread for 7 days, the other says not to eat any bread or grains until the offering is made. If the offering isn't made until the 2nd day of Unleavened bread, how can we rectify eating unleavened Bread on the 1st day?

The **Lexham English Septuagint** helps make this issue a little clearer. **Leviticus 23:14,** *And you will not eat bread and newly roasted grain until this very day, until* ***you yourselves*** *bring your gifts near to your God, it is a perpetual law throughout your generations in all your settlements.*

Prior to the public offering of the Wave Sheaf, no fresh barley could be reaped or cut, sold or used in the land. The key word being fresh, the unleavened bread on the 1st day was from the prior harvest. Verse 14 simply says, "bread or newly roasted grains," implying bread means unleavened products from old grain. In Joshua chapter 5 we read the following, *11 The day after the Passover, they ate of the produce of the land, unleavened bread, and roasted grain. 12 The manna stopped the day after they ate from the produce of the land, and the children of Israel no longer had manna. That year they ate what the land of Canaan yielded.* (**Joshua 5;11-12**)

Once the new grain was sanctified then offered by the priest, that's when the children of Israel began eating from the new crops, and the manna was stopped. The manna nourished them through the 1st day of Unleavened Bread, just as the past annual harvest did in the subsequent years.

The children were to remove the leaven from their homes, leaving only unleavened bread for the children of Israel to consume.

As a side note, It's interesting we are told to bring for ourselves as a Wave Sheaf offering. Churches have taught in the past there is nothing for the people to do for the Wave Sheaf, but scriptures imply something different. The children of Israel in the past, would have brought their own Wave Sheaf offering to the temple on the 2nd day of Passover. It would be the offering of the first fruits from their harvest to be accepted by the Eternal. Examine the following verse in **Numbers 15: 17-21,** *The Lord spoke to Moses, saying: 18 Speak to the Israelites and say to them: After **you** come into the land to which I am bringing you, 19. whenever **you** eat of the bread of the land, **you** shall present a donation to the Lord. 20. From **your** first batch of dough you shall present a loaf as a donation; you shall present it just as **you** present a donation from the threshing floor. 21. Throughout **your** generations **you** shall give to the Lord a donation from the first of **your** batch of dough.*

How often did YOU count where the word, "you" is used? According to Alfred Edersheim's book, "The Temple, Its Ministry and Services" those individual offerings would have been brought to the Temple and given to the Priest. We have lost a lot of the understanding and symbolism behind the Wave

Sheaf offerings and we are now following the gods of Egypt once again by observing the Christian Pentecost.

Below is a graph visually displaying the comparison between the two scenarios of applying the ordinances stipulated in both Lev. 6 & 14, note how they affect the way we observe the days of Unleavened Bread.

Comparison between the two scenarios: (7th day weekly Sabbath vs 16th of ABIB / AVIV)

1) Wave Sheaf offered after 1st Day of Unleavened Bread on the 16th Abib / Aviv

Monday	Tuesday	Wednesday	Thursday	Friday	Sabbath	Sunday	Monday
1st Day UNLB 15th	Wave Sheaf 16th NEW CROP	OK TO EAT BREAD	OK TO EAT BREAD	OK TO EAT BREAD	OK TO EAT BREAD	21ST Last Day UNLB	
OLD GRAIN							
Day 1	Day 2	Day 3	Day 4	Day 5	Day 6	Day 7	

2) Wave Sheaf offered after the weekly 7th Day Sabbath, offered on Sunday

Monday	Tuesday	Wednesday	Thursday	Friday	Sabbath	Sunday	Monday
1st Day UNLB 15th	NO EATING OF BREAD	NO EATING OF BREAD	NO EATING OF BREAD	NO EATING OF BREAD	NO EATING OF BREAD	Wave Sheaf Offered. NEW GRAIN Last Day UNLB	
OLD GRAIN							
Day 1	Day 2	Day 3	Day 4	Day 5	Day 6	Day 7	

Can YOU VISUALLY see how Lev. 23 : 6 & 14 ARE ONLY FULLFILLED if the Wave Sheaf is offered on the 16th of Abib / Aviv and the Omer count begins at this time , after the 1st day of Unleavened Bread

Law of Sacrifice

Deuteronomy 16:16 *"Three times a year all your males shall appear before the Eternal your God at the place which He chooses: at the Feast of Unleavened Bread, at the Feast of Weeks, and at the Feast of Booths; and they are not to appear before the Eternal empty-handed.*

Another important point to remember when considering the Messiah's sacrifice for mankind is the Law of Sacrifices.

Sacrifices in the Old Testament weren't trivial; they were seen as life and death and foreshadowed the Messiah's coming. The same can be said for the Wave Sheaf of the First Fruits; like all sacrifices, it is a sacrifice of harvested fruits of the land. The wave sheaf of barley had been plucked and essentially killed to offer before the Eternal, and subsequently, to be burned on the altar. The same is true for the unblemished lamb, slaughtered before being burned on the altar.

The Eternal will not ask for a live physical sacrifice; He commands against such practices. I understand Abraham was commanded to offer Issac on an altar as a sacrifice, but that was a test of Abraham's faith, and God held his hand back from completing the act.

In fact, after the test, God said this to Abraham in **Genesis 22:12**, *Now I know that you fear God, because you have not withheld from me your son, your only son.*

The Bible's instructions to the children of Israel are clear on how sacrifices are to be offered to God.

Leviticus. 1:5 " *And they shall kill the young bull before the Eternal;"*

Leviticus 1:11 " *and they shall kill it on the north side of the altar before the Eternal."*

Leviticus 1:15 *"and the priest shall carry it to the altar and wring off the head." (birds head)*

Every sacrifice must be a dead thing before its blood is used or parts placed on the altar as a sacrifice.

Leviticus 18:21 *"And you shall not let any of your descendants pass through the fire to Molech"* which did require living sacrifices, usually that of young children. (NKJ).

The Bible expressly condemns sacrificing live children to Moloch or for any other reason. Life is to be held sacred, and children are a blessing sent from the Eternal, not to be discarded for purposes of a sinful nature.

Keeping with contextual honesty, when we consider the First Fruits' or Wave Sheaf offerings, they are dead offerings made to the Eternal. Those plants and animals destined for sacrifice were immediately offered after harvesting. No priest or living person, for that matter, would conceive of waiting three days after harvesting to offer the sacrifice to the Eternal.

Once something is killed as a sacrifice, it must immediately be offered to God because if you wait, it becomes tainted and defiles those things around it.

Leviticus 2:11-12, *'No grain offering, which you bring to the Eternal, shall be made with leaven, for you shall not offer up in smoke any leaven or any honey as an offering by fire to the Eternal. 12 As an offering of first fruits you shall bring them to the Eternal, but they shall not ascend as a soothing aroma on the altar.*

Death begins an immediate leavening process of the body where bacteria breaks down the flesh. Those who believe the First Fruits occurred on a Sunday are a symbolic offering of the Messiah three days past His death and are not considering the decaying body. I don't deny the Messiah had to be accepted by the Father as our Wave Sheaf offering, but we must consider the law of the Torah.

I also am aware of the verses in **Acts 13:34-37,** where it says, *As for the fact that He raised Him from the dead, never again to return to decay, He has spoken in this way: 'I will give you the holy and faithful mercies of David.' 35 Therefore, He also says in another Psalm: 'You will not allow Your Holy One to undergo decay.' 36 For David, after he had served God's purpose in his own generation, fell asleep, and was buried among his fathers and underwent decay; 37 but He whom God raised did not undergo decay.*

With scriptures stating the Messiah's body escaped decay one might think that nullifies the law of sacrifice and it was possible to wait three days later for him to become the Wave Sheaf offering on Sunday. But, even though His body didn't decay it doesn't mean the laws of God can be transgressed.

It's clear the Messiah died on the 14th and was buried near or on the 15th as our symbolic Passover Lamb. Looking back at that first Passover in **Exodus 12:10** there is a clue we may have neglected to pick up on until the timing of the Wave Sheaf became controversial. **Exodus 12:10-11**, *And you shall not leave any of it over until morning, **but whatever is left of it until morning, you shall completely burn with fire**. 11 Now you shall eat it in this way: with your garment belted around your waist, your sandals on your feet, and your staff in your hand; and you shall eat it in a hurry—it is the Lord's Passover.*

Whatever was let on the morning of the 15th was to be burned by fire where no remnants were to remain of the body. Why? Why was it necessary to totally consume the sacrifice leaving no trace?

Before the Harvesting of Israel from the world (Egypt) began, the Passover had to be completed. The blood of the

Messiah bought and protected Israel on their journey the next 50 days to Mt. Sini where a covenant was ratified between the two (**Exodus 19 ref.**).

Keep in mind the Wave Sheaf hadn't even been given at this point as a rite the children of Israel were to perform yearly. This tells me two things; one, Passover was and is about the blood, **Exodus 12:13** *"The blood shall be a sign for you on the houses where you live"* and we also know that life is in the blood **Leviticus 17:11 ref.**

The second part of the Passover had to be completed before the Wave Sheaf could occur. **Joshua 5:10-12,** *While the sons of Israel camped at Gilgal they celebrated the Passover on the evening of the fourteenth day of the month on the desert plains of Jericho. 11. Then on the day after thse Passover, on that very day, they ate some of the produce of the land, unleavened cakes and roasted grain. 12.* ***And the manna ceased on the day after they had eaten some of the produce of the land****, so that the sons of Israel no longer had manna, but they ate some of the yield of the land of Canaan during that year.*

Add these elements together and the picture becomes clearer. The Passover was about our sins and the Messiah's blood redeeming mankind. The Wave Sheaf, a totally different offering (which included a lamb as a sacrifice) was symbolic of the gathering of new creatures in Christ. The Passover service had to end before the Wave Sheaf ceremony could begin, they were back to back symbolic offerings.

Another critical point to reckon concerning the Wave Sheaf being the Messiah is that He was again a living entity three days later when He met with Mary. If he wasn't living, why make this comment to Mary? **John 20:17,** *Jesus said to her, "Stop clinging to Me, for I have not yet ascended to the*

Father; but go to My brothers and say to them, 'I am ascending to My Father and your Father, and My God and your God.

It's been suggested the Messiah wouldn't let Mary touch him before ascending to the Father because He still had not been accepted as the Wave Sheaf offering. Meaning He was alive, not as a human being, but able to take physical form.

It's not entirely clear why the Messiah made an appearance before ascending to the Father. It's my thought, and you can plug your ears, or skip over this portion if you don't care to know what I think. It's my view, the Messiah needed to take His rightful place next to the Father on the throne in heaven showing the universe he had fulfilled His part of the plan. **Revelation 3:21, NASB**: *The one who overcomes, I will grant to him to sit with Me on My throne, as I also overcame and sat with My Father on His throne.*

God's chosen are the second harvest to come, and we too, are to overcome as he did, fulfilling our role in His holy plan of salvation.

It makes all the sense in the world, the Messiah was physically and symbolically offered and accepted as the Wave Sheaf offering on the 16th, the 2nd Day of Unleavened Bread. Only at this time does He fulfill all the requirements of a sacrifice made to the Eternal. Consider this, If He wasn't dead when sacrificed, can the Messiah be our savior?

If the Wave Sheaf had been on the Sabbath day, the actual cutting and preparing of the barley would have taken place at the beginning of that weekly Sabbath, another violation of the laws.

Back to my original question, why did the Messiah supposedly wait to be accepted as the wave sheaf by the Father when clearly the narrative says the cutting and presentation should have occurred at the beginning of the 2nd day of

Passover, the evening of the Sabbath, if this narrative is accurate?

I've given my supposition but, the problem with a lot of others assumptions about the Wave Sheaf is the Messiah rose on Sunday morning. The scripture makes it clear this is also untrue.

John 20:1, *Now on the first day of the week Mary Magdalene came early to the tomb, while it was still dark, and saw the stone already removed from the tomb.*

The Messiah was clearly gone before morning came, and the sun rose. Most folks adhering to the three days and nights narrative recognize that the Messiah's resurrection would have occurred as the Sabbath ended that week.

Taking that into account, I would like to ask another question, "what did the Messiah do from the time He was resurrected to the time He met with Mary in the garden the next day?"

Once dead and offered up, that is the ceremonial conclusion to a sacrifice. If we say the Wave Sheaf offering is on that Sunday, consider all requirements had already been fulfilled days before that point. Only the counting of the omer would have been left and that would have begun on the 3rd day of Passover. If you're still cutting the puzzle pieces to make them fit the picture, please stop.

Symbolism of the First Fruits

Psalm 24:24, *The earth is the Eternal's, and all it contains, The world, and those who live in it.*

All the first fruits are the Eternals, it's the law of sacrifices for those called God's own. The first and best belongs to him and is to be given to him.

The word first fruits is mentioned 32 times in the Bible. The first mention of the word is found in **Exodus 23:14-17**, *"Three times a year you shall celebrate a feast to Me. 15 You shall keep the Feast of Unleavened Bread; for seven days you are to eat unleavened bread, as I commanded you, at the appointed time in the month of Abib, for in that month you came out of Egypt. And no one is to appear before Me empty-handed. 16 Also you shall keep the Feast of the Harvest of the first fruits of your labors from what you sow in the field; also the Feast of the Ingathering at the end of the year when you gather in the fruit of your labors from the field. 17 Three times a year all your males shall appear before the Eternal God.*

Those in the past and present calling themselves God's holy people are told to celebrate the Festival of Harvest with their first fruits. By doing this we honor God and also this is a reminder, we are his first fruits. Verse 19 of the same chapter says, *19 "You shall bring the choice first fruits of your soil into the house of the Eternal your God.*

How do we reconcile the two together with the "Wave Sheaf" offering and Firstfruits? What does it symbolize and represent? Notice it's a sheaf of the "First Fruits" offered to God before the Israelites can harvest one stalk of grain from their fields in the spring.

God commands, *"And ye shall eat neither bread, nor parched corn, nor green ears" – that is, produce from the new harvest – "until the self same day that ye have brought an offering unto your God: it shall be a STATUTE FOR EVER throughout your generations in all your dwellings"* (**Leviticus 23:14**).

Paul writes to Christians in Rome, saying, *"For we know that the whole creation groaneth and travaileth in pain together until now. And not only they, but ourselves also, which have the FIRSTFRUITS OF THE SPIRIT, even we ourselves groan within ourselves, waiting for the adoption, to wit, the redemption of our body"* (**Romans 8:23**).

But this isn't the first fruit represented by the wave sheaf representing the Messiah. Yes, God's people are also first fruits but not before Christ…look what it says in 1 **Corinthians 15:20-24;** b*ut the fact is, Christ has been raised from the dead, the first fruits of those who are asleep. 21 For since by a man death came, by a man also came the resurrection of the dead. 22 For as in Adam all die, so also in Christ all will be made alive. 23 But each in his own order: Christ the firstfruits, after that those who are Christ's at His coming, 24 then comes the end, when He hands over the kingdom to our God and Father, when He has abolished all rule and all authority and power*

The other notable aspect of the symbolic meaning of the Wave Sheaf , it was represented by an omer of barley, which would be the unleavened Messiah. The first omer presented before God on the 16th is symbolically the Messiah. The Messiah was unleavened just as the offering for the wave sheaf was done on the 2nd day of Unleavened Bread.

This is in stark contrast to the offerings to be made in the celebration of Feast of Weeks. **Leviticus 23:17-20,** *You shall bring in from your dwelling places **two loaves of bread** as a* *wave offering, made of two-tenths of an ephah; they shall be of a fine flour, baked with leaven as first fruits to the Eternal. 18 Along with the bread you shall present seven one-year-old male lambs without defect, and a bull of the herd and two rams; they are to be a burnt offering to the Eternal, with their grain offering and their drink offerings, an offering by fire of a soothing aroma to the Eternal. 19 You shall also offer one male goat as a sin offering, and two male lambs one year old as a sacrifice of peace offerings. 20 The priest shall then wave them with the bread of the first fruits as a wave offering with two lambs before the Eternal; they are to be holy to the Eternal for the priest.*

There is such a huge difference between these two offerings, where both are called First Fruits; one has to wonder what they mean.

Here are the differences in offerings compared to one another.

Wave Sheaf Offering of first fruits	Feast of Weeks Offering of first fruits
A burnt offering of 1 Lamb	A burnt offering of 7 lambs, 1 bull, two rams
2-tenths of 1 Ephah flour unleavened mixed with oil.	2 Loaves made of two-tenths of an ephah; they shall be of fine flour, baked with leaven
Drink offering of a fourth of a hin of wine	An unknown amount of drink offering

Added Peace Offering

1 male goat, 2 male lambs

14 Until this very day, until you have brought in the offering of your God, you shall eat neither bread nor roasted grain nor new produce. It is to be a permanent statute throughout your generations in all your dwelling places.	*20 The priest shall then wave them with the bread of the first fruits as a wave offering with two lambs before the Eternal; they are to be holy to the Lord for the priest.*

It's safe to assume the first Wave Sheaf or offering of the First Fruit is symbolic of the Messiah and the first omer presented before the heavenly host. The 50th omer offering was the Feast of Weeks and is symbolic of his church's ingathering. Not just the New Testament church but all his people from the beginning of His creation. As a reminder of **1 Corinthians 15:20-24**, *But the fact is, Christ has been raised from the dead, **the first fruits** of those who are asleep. 21. For since by a man* *death came, by a man also came the resurrection of the dead. 22. For as in Adam all die, so also in Christ, all will be made alive. 23. But each in his own order: **Christ the first fruits**, after that those who are **Christ's at His coming**, 24. **Then comes the end**, when He hands over the kingdom to our God and Father, when He has abolished all rule and all authority and power*

I don't mean to be redundant, but we must be aware of the order of things given to us in the Eternals celebration of His Holy convocations to understand them completely.

I realize I can be annoyingly repetitive when going back to the point about counting seven weeks (Sabbaths) to arrive upon the proper day of celebration, Feast of Weeks, or Pentecost. It's important to observe God's commanded festivals on the correct days when the Eternal in heaven observes them.

I use the example of Atonement and the Priest going into the Holy of Holies on the wrong day. It didn't matter if it was by accident, miscalculation, or if the Priest had a good heart and meant well; he died on the spot. We are shown by this example how seriously God takes celebration on the correct days.

In **Hebrews 8:4-5**, it states, *Now if He were on earth, He would not be a priest at all, since there are those who offer the gifts according to the Law; 5. Who serve a copy and shadow of the heavenly things, just as Moses was warned by God when he was about to erect the tabernacle; for, "See," He says, "that you make all things by the pattern which was shown to you on the mountain."*

If the law is a shadow of good things to come (**Heb. 10:1**), and Temple artifacts and procedures were to be duplicates of those in heaven, shouldn't we be more precise about how and when we observe the Holy days (Lev. 23 Ref)?

Connection with Harvest

1 Corinthians 15:20, *But the fact is, Christ has been raised from the dead, the first fruits of those who are asleep.*

The symbolic meaning of the Wave Sheaf has always been one of harvest; my observation leads me to believe we in God's church have sidestepped that part of the wave sheaf ritual. There is a very clear correlation between harvest, resurrections, and counting the omer. Christ was the wave sheaf offering and 1st omer who was crucified and offered up. Fifty days later, the celebration of the first fruits occurred. Two thousand years later, we may not have a complete understanding of the significance of these harvests, but they had real, tangible meanings to the disciples.

If, by supposition, the Wave Sheaf and counting are to begin the day after the weekly Sabbath that year, then you would have a total of 53 days from the time of harvest to the Feast of Weeks. By all accounts, including **Leviticus 23:11-16**, it was to be 50 days after the sacrifice. This symbolic difference cannot be rectified by counting from the weekly Sabbath after a Sunday resurrection taking into account the words of the Messiah, *"he would be in the tomb three days and nights."*

Fifty represents the year of Jubilee, the giving of the law to his people, the outpouring of God's holy spirit, and salvation for God's people. This can only be achieved by the death of the sacrifice and not by the spiritual resurrection 3 days later, hence the 53 days as opposed to 50 days.

It's by the Messiah's death we obtain salvation. He died for our sins, as the scriptures repeatedly state.
Romans 5:8, ESV *But God shows his love for us in that while we were still sinners, Christ died for us.*

1 Peter 3:18 ESV *For Christ also suffered once for sins, the righteous for the unrighteous, that he might bring us to God, being put to death in the flesh but made alive in the spirit,*
Hebrews 9:22 ESV *Indeed, under the law almost everything is purified with blood, and without the shedding of blood there is no forgiveness of sins.*
1 John 2:2 ESV *He is the propitiation for our sins, and not for ours only but also for the sins of the whole world.*

I have found no passage in the Old or New Testament that says the Messiah was resurrected for our sins. Placing emphasis on the Messiah's resurrection as opposed to His death is a mistake when establishing a correct timeline.

Another way to look at this would be God is planting and harvesting, beginning in **Genesis 8:22**, where it says, *While the earth remaineth, seedtime and harvest, and cold and heat, and summer and winter, and day and night shall not cease.*

One might be inclined to interpret these as dual meanings. Aside from the obvious, another definition could be as long as there is an earth, God will harvest His chosen from every conceivable condition one can imagine. This is a key to understanding the celebration of the Feast of Weeks or Pentecost. The Messiah used the analogy of harvest several times concerning salvation.

Matthew 9:36-38, *Seeing the crowds, He felt compassion for them, because they were distressed and downcast, like sheep without a shepherd. 37 Then He said to His disciples, "The harvest is plentiful, but the workers are few. 38 Therefore, plead with the Eternal of the harvest to send out workers into His harvest."*

Also in, **John 4:35-38**, *Do you not say, 'There are still four months, and then comes the harvest'? Behold, I tell you, raise your eyes and observe the fields, that they are white for harvest.*

36. Already the one who reaps is receiving wages and is gathering fruit for eternal life, so that the one who sows and the one who reaps may rejoice together. 37. For in this case the saying is true: 'One sows and another reaps.' 38. I sent you to reap that for which you have not labored; others have labored, and you have come into their labor."

The book of James illustrates a very distinctive connection with God, the harvest and salvation. **James 5:7,** *Be patient, therefore, brothers, until the coming of the Eternal. See how the farmer waits for the precious fruit of the earth, being patient about it, until it receives the early and the late rains.*

Even the definitions are in opposition to one another. The Greek word Pentecost means to count 50 days, and the term Feast of Weeks means to count 7 Sabbaths or weeks.

The grain harvest in that region of the world lasted seven weeks and was a season of gladness (**Deuteronomy. 16:9, Isaiah 11:2**). It began with the harvesting of the barley during the Passover or Feast of Weeks and ended with the harvesting of the wheat at Pentecost or Feast of Weeks, the wheat being the last grain to ripen. Pentecost was thus the concluding festival of the grain harvest, just as the eighth Day of Tabernacles was the concluding festival of the fruit harvest.

According to **Exodus 34:18-26**, the Feast of Weeks is the second of the three festivals to be celebrated by all males at the sanctuary. They are required to bring to the sanctuary *"the first-fruits of wheat harvest," "the first-fruits of thy labors which thou hast sown in the field."*

Counting the Omer

Leviticus 23:15, *'You shall also count for yourselves from the day after the Sabbath, from the day when you brought in the sheaf of the wave offering; there shall be seven complete Sabbaths.*

I have no doubt that the 50 days leading up to the celebration of the feast of Weeks are significant in a major way. What that is, I can't be as sure of as our friend Mr. Dankenbring is in his presentations of "counting the omer."

Our friend, William F. Dankenbring, has advanced the idea, we must acknowledge that in some fashion the counting of the omer each and every one of the fifty days leading up to the Feast of Weeks.

This is his volition in his own words, "The counting of the Omer" from Pesach (Passover) to Shavuot (Pentecost) is a process – a daily task – that reflects like a mirror our spiritual lives. If we are not counting the Omer as God tells us to do, it is reflective of the fact that we are not overcoming sin and temptations, and distractions in our lives. If we fail to count one day, but repent, and begin counting from that time, then God forgives us, and we go onward and forward. But it is better if we are faithful from beginning to end."

I can't disagree that the omer is a reflection of our journey out of Egypt (the world), but how are we to count the omer properly? I see no dictates to do anything special other than count the days. My next thought, it's an effort every day of the year to separate ourselves from sin. So, counting these 50 days should reflect back to a place in our lives where a change took place....that means something to God.

It's my own assertion counting the omer is a way of marking the time we are to become one with the Messiah. He began the count to his marriage, culminating 50 days later with matrimony with his bride. It's looking to the day we are resurrected into the Kingdom of God as partners in a covenant.

God's people are bound by a covenant of marriage to the creator of the universe; that is clear. We are to prepare for that meeting below the mountain during this period.

Mr. Dankenbring also asserts, "Each day of the remaining forty-nine-day Omer count is like a building block to salvation." He also asserts, "It is a tool to develop and grow in spiritual maturity so that we are ready when Christ comes so that we will be a pure and perfect Bride."

As I said, I have no quarrel with what he said, only what actual meaningful way this is done. Is it through prayer, meditation, going out, and practicing what we deem is slated for that particular day?

Is it simply a reflection on our spiritual lives that we might spend an extra minute to two on each of those 50 days?

One could create their own tradition of reflecting on God and their journey with him in this world. All traditions aren't bad, but I would simply caution about how dogmatic we become with any man-made traditions.

I see Passover as a special event where the Messiah pays the dowry for his bride (the church) with his blood, and the Feast of Weeks or Pentecost, where God's people make a commitment to sealing the covenant and receiving his blessings in the form of His Holy Spirit.

The beauty and symmetry of the church, the Messiah's bride, have escaped the secular world. The holy days correlate with the Father's and Messiah's mission to build upon the spiritual family.

One more concern folks may wonder about that needs to be addressed. In the King James Version, along with some other translations, **Lev. 23:15** says, *"And ye shall count unto you from the morrow after the sabbath, from the day that ye brought the sheaf of the wave offering;* **seven sabbaths** *shall be complete:"*

This is somewhat incorrect considering most other translations quote the same verse, *"15 And from the day after the sabbath, from the day on which you bring the sheaf of the elevation offering, you shall count off seven weeks; they shall be complete." (**New Revised Standard Version Catholic Edition**)*.

I would have you take notice; I quoted from a catholic version of their Bibles to show the true intent of this verse…. if they can get it right, anyone can. There is a big difference in how you interpret this verse. If you say 7 Sabbaths must be complete, you are following the Greek Pentecostal crowd to establish a Sunday observance. On the other hand, by saying count after the 1st day of Unleavened Bread, and 7 full weeks must pass, the proper fulfillment of the feast of weeks is therefore established. After all, It is called the Feast of Weeks and not the feast of Sabbaths. Upholding all of God's ordinances leads us to count correctly and not take away or add to the words of the Torah.

What is Pentecost?

We've covered many aspects of the meaning of the Wave Sheaf, the omer, first fruits, and the celebration of the Feast of Weeks up to this point in the book.

But the mainstream churches today don't recognize the term Feast of Weeks…. they see this celebration as the Birth of the New Testament church, calling it "Pentecost."

But what is the Christian definition of the word Pentecost other than "count fifty?"

For that, we need to reference biblical dictionaries, like **Vine's Expository Dictionary of New Testament** Words by Hendrickson under Pentecost. *an adjective denoting "fiftieth," is used as a noun, with "day" understood, i.e., the "fiftieth"* **day after the Passover, counting from the second day of the Feast,** *Acts 2:1; 20:16; 1 Cor. 16:8. For the divine instructions to Israel see Exod. 23:16; 34:22; Lev. 23:15-21; Num. 28:26-31; Deut. 16:9-11.*

I know, I'm shocked as well; Vine's definition of New testament words begins the definition of the word as saying it was understood you begin counting on the 2nd day of the Feast. What feast? The 2nd day of Unleavened Bread is the only feast that occurs around that time.

Okay, that must have been a fluke; let's try another biblical Dictionary; this time, we'll look at Donald T. Kauffman's Dictionary of religious terms. *Pentecost fiftieth 1. feast of weeks celebrated seven weeks after* **Passover** *in recognition of the grain harvest and its ingathering.*

Initially, that definition didn't give me what I was looking for, a new testament definition of the word Pentecost. But it did support Vines' version; it did go on to say Christians observe Pentecost seven weeks after the day of Easter, which I find interesting. Subsequently, I examined Montgomery F. Essig's "**The Comprehensive Analysis of the Bible**," which says pretty much the same thing. Jews count fifty days after **Passover**. Christians on the other hand, begin counting fifty days after Easter. **Wycliffe's bible Commentary** was the same, as well as **Unger's Bible Dictionary** in supporting the fact we count from the 2nd day of Passover.

I almost forgot the most important reference to understanding words in the Bible, **Hebrew or Greek, and that's Strong's concordance**. The word Pentecost is the *Greek 4005. pentekoste pen-tay-kos-tay' feminine of the ordinal of 4004; fiftieth (2250 being implied) from Passover, i.e. the festival of "Pentecost":*--Pentecost.

It's the same word used in Acts 2, where it says, *When the day of Pentecost had come, they were all together in one place. (Acts 2:1)*

Strong's didn't say Easter or count from the weekly Sabbath? If Pentecost is supposed to be a Christian celebration, why does Strong's say fifty days after Passover? It's beginning to feel a lot like mixing oil and water; and as we know, they'll never come together.

Is there a difference in the definitions of Pentecost whether you are a Hebrew or gentile? Perhaps that's true in the religious world, but not with God, there is only one way to count, and that's from the 2nd day of Passover.

I did see a pattern develop while combing through dictionaries. If they were biblical dictionaries, they begin by saying count from Passover; if they were from a secular viewpoint, the emphasis was on counting from Easter. The vaunted 11th edition of the Encyclopedia Britannica began its oratory by saying originally, *"it was a celebration of the Jews."*

My impression was, "don't all Christian views of the Old Testament begin with that thought?"

Sadly, the Christian version of Pentecost is also prominent in the Churches of Gods'; nearly everyone counts from Easter winding up on a Pentecostal Sunday celebration every single year.

I remember attending a summer Bible study seminar our church organization hosted one year. One of the prominent minters saw a vine's Dictionary on my desk and tapped on the book, warning me some references were unreliable.

After seeing the definition of Pentecost in the pages of Vine's, I wonder if that wasn't the emphasis of his warning? The biblical definition flies in the face of the Churches of God's Statement of beliefs. I'm sorry if that offends some, but whether you agree or not this has to be said.

The Christian celebration of Pentecost all but ends with a special service on Sunday. In contrast, the celebration of the Feast of Weeks or Shavuot was much more extensive since given by the Eternal. It all begins with the presentation of the 1st omer on the 2nd day of Passover.

Conclusion

Acts 26:14, *And when we had all fallen to the ground, I heard a voice saying to me in the Hebrew dialect, 'Saul, Saul, why are you persecuting Me? It is hard for you to kick against the goads.'*

Going back to the beginning of the book, I said the overall premise was to come as far out of the world as possible. There are irreconcilable differences between the Christian and Hebrew interpretations of these two events. One has to ask if you are starting the count from a pagan ritual (Easter) to land upon one of God's holy days. Doesn't that fail the smell test just a little?

When do God's people ever begin anything with paganism as the basis for finding God's will in these matters?

If that is possible, why not follow their interpretation of the day of the week in which God's people should go to church? Why not accept the holidays they celebrate, like Easter and Christmas? If we just succumbed to the desire to be like the rest of the world, our little church would grow by leaps and bounds with new converts. All we have to do is accept what Christian doctrines they advocate. I have no ill will toward Christians; after all, some of my best friends are Christians. But they adhere to a set of principles and doctrines that contradict the Bible. Our beliefs are an extension of what and who we are. They tell others in the world what rules we follow in our lives, and the Messiah said, in **John 14:15**, *If you love me, keep my commandments.*

I guess it's time to remind everyone just how popular the Messiah was. He was so popular that they put Him to death for exposing the lies of the religious world.

Let me add my personal touch, the Feast of Weeks or Pentecost is not a Christian festival when observed correctly. It is one of God's festivals to be honored the way God instructed. To let a foreign entity, no matter how good-willed, tell God's people how to observe His days is an abomination.

I agree there isn't always a clear and exact answer for every question but finding the proper application for scripture begins with a good investigation. It also means leaving agendas behind in the world and searching for God's truths and not man's version of the truth. In **Deuteronomy 29:29** *"The secret things belong to the Eternal our God, but the things revealed belong to us and to our sons forever, so that we may follow all the words of this Law.*

We have now come full circle and are back to the beginning of our premises. Will we walk away from the world? Will we be willing to forsake all others and follow only the true creator, God? Are we done participating in the evil of the harlot mentioned in Revelation 17?

The first fruits of the Feast of Weeks or Shavuot are the future bride of the Messiah. The offerings made that day are for our sins and a peace offering to reconcile us back into favor with the Bridegroom (please read my book, The Bride), for a deeper understanding of the Bride & bridegroom from **Revelation 19 Ref**. Let that be the celebration of life and spirit as we assemble together this year at the Feast of Weeks, counting fifty days from the 2nd day of Passover.

Quick Scriptural References

Page 2. Luke 8:17, Revelation 18:4), Proverbs 14:12,
Page 3. Proverbs 16:25
Page 6. 1 John 4:1, Leviticus 23:11 & 15, Leviticus 23:11
Page 7. Leviticus 23:11 & 15, Leviticus 23:11
Page 8. Leviticus 23:11 & 15, Leviticus 23:11,
Page 9. Genesis 2:2-3
Page 10. Exodus 20:8-11
Page 11. Leviticus 23: 11 & 15, Leviticus 23:1-3, Leviticus 23:4-8
Page 12. Leviticus 23:9-22
Page 13. Leviticus 23:23-35, Leviticus 23:26-32,
Page 14. Leviticus 23;11
Page 15. Strong's Hebrew 7676,
Page 16. Exodus 23:10-11, Leviticus 23:33-36,
Page 17. Leviticus 23:41-44, Exodus 31:12-17, Ezekiel 20:12, Leviticus 23:11
Page 19. Mark 2:27, Strong's Greek #4521,
Page 20. Matthew 12:1-2, John 19: 31
Page 21. Matthew 12:38-40
Page 22. Luke 23:55-56, Mark's 16:1
Page 23. Acts 9:37, John 19:40
Page 25. Proverbs 27:17,
Page 26. Joshua 5:11, Leviticus 23:14
Page 27. Leviticus 23:15, Mat.12:1, 11; Mark 1:21; 2:23; 3:2; Luke 4:16; 13:10;
        Acts 13:14.; 16:13
Page 28. I Corinthians 16:2, Mat.28:1; Mark 16:2; Luke 24:1; John 20:1, 19; Acts 20:7
Page 30. 1 Timothy 6:10, Leviticus 23:11
Page 31. Matthew 22:24-29
Page 32. Acts 23:7-8
Page 33. Matthew 3:7-9,
Page 34: Matthew 23:1-3
Page 37. Romans 3:2
Page 39. Galatians 1:8, Leviticus 23:11
Page 40. Leviticus 23:11
Page 41. Leviticus 23:11, Encyclopedia Britannica
Page 43. Wycliff commentary Leviticus 23:10-11
Page 44. Lev. 23:11, Josephus, Antiquities 3.250-251, in Josephus IV Jewish Antiquities
Page 46. Lev. 23:11, Jousha 5:11, Page 38. C.F. Keil, D.D. and F. Delitzsch, D.D.in Vol.
        one of the Pentateuch
Page 47. 2 Corinthians 13:1, Leviticus 23:24, 32, 39, The testimony of Josephus (antiq.
        3.248-249).
Page 48. Leviticus 7:30, Exodus 9:22–26; Leviticus 8:25–29, Leviticus 23:11
Page 49. Jeremiah 10:2
Page 51. John 18:28,
John 52:31 (Sanhedrin, Mishnah IV.1; cf. Deuteronomy 21:23, (The Jewish War, VI.9.3).

Page 53. Genesis 1:2-3, Genesis (1:8; 1:13; 1:19; 1:23; 1:31, Leviticus 23:32
Page 55. Joshua 5:10-12
Page 56. John 6;35, Matthew 5:17-20, Deuteronomy 4:2, Revelation 22:18-19, Matthew 9:35 Luke 24:44, Matthew 15:7, and Matthew 5;17
Page 58. omer (approx. 14 cups) log (slightly more than 0.5 liters (0.14 U.S. gallon), of oil.
Page 59. Acts 2
Page 60. Deuteronomy 16:4, Leviticus 23:6, Leviticus 23:14
Page 61. Exodus 12:15-16, Deuteronomy 16:4, Lexham English Septuagint
Page 62. Joshua 5;11-12, Numbers 15: 17-21
Page 64. Deuteronomy 16:16, Genesis 22:12, Leviticus. 1:5, Leviticus 1:11, Leviticus 1:15
Page 65. Leviticus 2:11-12,
Page 66. Acts 13:34-37, Exodus 12:10, Exodus 12:10-11,
Page 67.Exodus 19 ref, Exodus 12:13, Joshua 5:10-12, John 20:17
Page 68. Revelation 3:21
Page 69. John 20:1
Page 70. Psalm 24:24, Exodus 23:14-17,
Page 71. Leviticus 23:14, Romans 8:2, 1 Corinthians 15:20-24, Leviticus 23:17-20
Page 73. 1 Corinthians 15:20-24
Page 74. Hebrews 8:4-5, Heb. 10:1
Page 75. 1 Corinthians 15:20, Leviticus 23:11-16, Romans 5:8,
Page 76. 1 Peter 3:18, Hebrews 9:22, Genesis 8:22, Matthew 9:36-38, John 4:35-38
Page 77. James 5:7, Deuteronomy. 16:9, Isaiah 11:2, Exodus 34:18-26
Page 78. Leviticus 23:15
Page 80. Leviticus 23: (New Revised Standard Version Catholic Edition).
Page 81. Vine's Expository Dictionary of New Testament Acts 2:1; 20:16; 1 Cor. 16:8. Exod. 23:16; 34:22; Lev. 23:15-21; Num. 28:26-31; Deut. 16:9-11. The Comprehensive Analysis of the Bible, Wycliffe's bible
Page 82. Unger's Bible Dictionary, Greek, and that's Strong's concordance #4005, Acts 2
Page 84. Acts 26:14, John 14:15
Page 85. Deuteronomy 29:29, Revelation 17, Revelation 19 Ref

Seasonal Calendar

Spring Feast

Year	Passover *	Unleavened Bread	Feast of Weeks
2023	April 5	April 6 – April 12	May 26
2024	April 23	April 24 – April 30	June 13
2025	April 13	April 14 – April 20	June 3
2026	April 3	April 4 – April 10	May 24
2027	April 22	April 23 – April 29	June 12
2028	April 10	April 11 – April 17	May 31
2029	April 29	April 30 – May 6	June 19
2030	April 18	April 19 – April 25	June 8

Fall Feast

Year	Trumpets	Atonement	FOT	LGD
2023	Sept 17	Sept 26	Oct 1 - Oct 7	Oct 8
2024	Oct 5	Oct 14	Oct 19 – Oct 25	Oct 26
2025	Sept 24	Oct 3	Oct 8 – Oct 14	Oct 15
2026	Sept 13	Sept 22	Sept 27 – Oct 3	Oct 4
2027	Oct 2	Oct 11	Oct 16 – Oct 22	Oct 23
2028	Sept 20	Sept 29	Oct 4 – Oct 10	Oct 11
2029	Oct 9	Oct 18	Oct 23 – Oct 29	Oct 30
2030	Sept 29	Oct 8	Oct 13 – Oct 19	Oct 20

Acronyms: FOT (Feast of Tabernacles, LGD (last Great Day).

• * means PASSOVER BEGINS AT SUNSET the evening before

- NEW MOONS are BIBLICAL (First Light) CRESCENT MOONS

- Stellarium Astronomy Software Program

Acronyms: FOT (Feast of Tabernacles), LGD (Last Great Day). UNLB (Unleavened Bread)

Other Publications from tomorrow's Church of God can be found on www.thetcog.com.

Email us at tomorrowtcog@gmail.com

Credits: I would like to give special credit to Billy and Julie Stefek, and Linda Boyd for their work in putting this information together.

Theodore Hawkins for his time creating Audio CDs.

Made in the USA
Monee, IL
23 January 2023

25728922R00056